The GC
HOW TO
BE A DIVA

GEMMA COLLINS

The GC

HOW TO BE A DIVA

Headline

First published in 2018
by HEADLINE PUBLISHING GROUP

1

Cataloguing in Publication Data is available from the British Library

Hardback ISBN 978 1 4722 5690 4
Trade paperback ISBN 978 1 4722 5692 8

Typeset in Chaparral Pro 12/20 by Jouve (UK), Milton Keynes

Printed and bound in Great Britain by Clays Ltd, Elcograf S.p.A.

Headline's policy is to use papers that are natural, renewable and recyclable
products and made from wood grown in well-managed forests and other
controlled sources. The logging and manufacturing processes are expected
to conform to the environmental regulations of the country of origin.

HEADLINE PUBLISHING GROUP
An Hachette UK Company
Carmelite House
50 Victoria Embankment
London
EC4Y 0DZ

www.headline.co.uk
www.hachette.co.uk

This book is dedicated to my mother,
Joan Collins,
the original diva

CONTENTS

INTRODUCTION

So girls, you all right darlings?

If you've bought this book, ordered it online, borrowed it from a library (if they still exist) or won it in a raffle, then congratulations. You have taken the first steps into a world where everything is fabulous. Men will fall at your feet, riches will be bestowed on you, you will have the biggest, bounciest hair ever and you will get what you want, whatever that is. You will be respected, adored, envied, and some people might get a little bit scared of you (but don't worry, it'll be because of their insecurities, not because you've turned ugly or anything). You will have more fun than you ever thought possible. Your life will also be filled with drama – but not the depressing type of drama like the stuff you see on

EastEnders; it will be the glamorous sort of drama like on *Desperate Housewives*. The reason for all of this is because you are about to become a diva. And that's a good thing, believe me.

My name is Gemma Collins, but I am more commonly known as 'The GC', one of our nation's diva icons. But then you already know that because you've bought this book, for which I salute you, because you didn't have to buy it. There were lots of other choices in the bookshop, or on Amazon or wherever. So let me reassure you that your hard-earned money has been well spent. You have made an investment in your future. If you were weighing up whether to buy this or some chick-lit novel, you're in luck, because I promise you, the next few hundred pages will be much more entertaining than that Sophie Kinsella you were considering instead. Let's face it, those kinds of books are all the same. Heroine is unfulfilled, heroine goes on journey, heroine finds man, tragedy happens, heroine finds herself, man saves her, they all live happy ever after. This book is different because you're the heroine and the journey you are about to embark upon is a journey of self-discovery. If Jackie Collins (rest in peace) did self-help, this is what she would have written. In fact – thanks to my psychic ability (more of that later) – I'm channelling Jackie as I type. Literally, there is Brentwood glamour dripping off my shellac onto the keys of my laptop as I write this.

So as the cover says, I'm a diva and I've earned my divaship through many years of hard work, hairdryers and broken hearts. I'm glitzy, gobby and so glamorous that I shit glitter. In fact I guess you could say that I am the 'every woman' Chaka Khan sings about who has the brains, the beauty and the booty. Don't get me wrong, though, I can be controversial sometimes: a bit like sequinned Marmite, you either love me or hate me. But you also love to hate me, and secretly you love me. Make sense? Don't worry, it will become clear later.

I am the big, brash, loud blonde one from *The Only Way Is Essex*, or *TOWIE* as it's now affectionately known, the best reality TV show around, obviously. For anyone unfortunate enough not to have seen *TOWIE* I'll give you a quick taster. It is a reality show that follows the lives and loves of a group of mainly young, glamorous people. It is set in and around a place called Brentwood in Essex. It is not a coincidence that Brentwood and Hollywood share the same last syllable. Brentwood is the Hollywood of the UK. It's jammed full of glam. Imagine if someone loaded a massive container ship full of sparkles, glamour, razzle-dazzle and the best gear the shops have to offer, then put it on a giant trailer, filled the petrol tank full of glitter and sent it hurtling round the M25 to ram-raid Essex. The result would be Brentwood. And that's where I call home.

I burst onto the nation's television screens in 2011 – before that I was a car dealer working in a Beamer showroom

('Beamer' is Essex for BMW). I had several other jobs before I became a full-time diva although, as you'll find out, I was always a diva and destined to be a star. I'd been waiting in the wings all my life and it is fair to say that when fame reared its head I grabbed it by the horns and milked its showbiz-filled udders.

I've always been a believer in making the most of what life has to offer and I've managed to use the fame that *TOWIE* gave me to go off on adventures that I never thought possible. Things just haven't been the same since I arrived, for me and for the rest of the world. I'm the one who lasted for three triumphant days in the jungle on *I'm a Celebrity Get Me Out of Here!* I'm the one who refused to do the tasks on *Celebrity Big Brother* (or took the executive decision that having my hair washed was more important than my team mates). I took the term 'stage diving' to a whole other level and cemented myself as the queen of the memes and a national treasure to boot. Plus I'm a ruthless business magnate (like a younger, beardless Alan Sugar in heels), a fashion designer and icon.

But there's another side to me too. I'm also a family-loving girl from Romford who loves her mates and girlie nights in but who is caught up in a life of glamour, excess and complicated love-life decisions. I'm the captain of my own ship. I don't answer to no one, but I've had my heart broken, my dreams crushed and my dress sense questioned. And I'm still standing, bigger and bolder than ever. Without being too modest,

I'm a legend. I've earned my diva stripes: I don't just play the diva game, I invented it.

So here I am, fingers dancing over my keyboard like Anton du Beke on E numbers, sharing my secrets with you, lucky reader. Grab yourself a cup of hot chocolate and some biccies, because over the next few hours, me and you are going on the literary version of a girls' spa weekend, where I'll be using words instead of face creams to make you the best version of yourself you can be.

I got asked to write this book because there just isn't enough glamour in the world at the moment and in my opinion, things need a bit of a shake up and a shake down. Everything is doom and gloom. I ain't the world's best expert on current affairs, but I watch *GMB* when I get the chance, and *Newsround* if I'm at a loss in the afternoon, and it seems to me that things have got to change. We've got some bloke with bad hair in America trying to mug people off, another bloke in a place called Korea with equally bad hair messing around and upsetting everyone and the queues at passport control in Malaga are going to get longer thanks to something called Brexit. Someone needs to take the initiative and brighten things up. And that falls to me and you. While you might not finish this book and immediately have the solution to the world's problems, if you follow my advice you'll have the solutions to *your* problems – and that's a start. You'll be fabulous and it's a diva's job to spread fabulousness. A recent study by the University of Essex found that there are not enough divas to do all the work needed (I might have made this up). Mariah is getting on a bit, Madonna has her hands full with all her adopted kids, so it falls to me to take the reins and start the diva revolution. And I want you to join me.

Over the following pages, I'm going to take you on a diva journey where I'll be your teacher, your mentor, your guru and guide. We'll explore the main themes of the diva lifestyle: attitude, appearance, men and social media. You'll learn what it means to be a diva, how to look like one, how to act like one and how to live like one. At the end of it all, you will be a fabulous diva like me and you'll have some make-up tips. You'll also learn some very juicy goss about me, my life, the men in my life, shock-induced urinary incontinence and some of the things I've done (including how I sustained an unsightly boob injury in front of Tom Daley while he was wearing a revealing pair of Speedos) (which could probably make a book on its own). So hold on to your extensions, because things are about to get interesting.

Chapter One

DIVA! IT'S A LIFESTYLE

Since the dawn of time, in the days of dinosaurs and the *Ice Age* movie franchise, before brow stencils, Samsung Galaxies and intimate waxes, there have always been women who are just a bit more fabulous than everyone else. Even when gossip was just a series of deep indecipherable grunts, there were cavewomen who worked out that they could create a decent updo using a fish skeleton and tree sap. There were others who discovered that mud cleared the complexion and smoothed away fine lines. Not to mention the prehistoric pioneer who, rather than use fur to make a coat, draped it nicely over a log in her cave and invented the throw. These were the world's first divas and history is littered with them.

For example, one of the originals was Boudicca, the warrior queen who came from near Essex. She had big hair and was one of the first Essex girls to appreciate a mean set of wheels. Her chariot had blades poking out of them, which must have caused havoc in the NCP Pay and Display. Then there was Elizabeth I. Not a looker by all accounts but still a lady who knew how to make the most of what she had, which was the whole of England, palaces and a crown. She had blokes eating out of her hand and, in what must be the first documented Deliveroo order, sent one, Walter Raleigh, all the way to America to get chips (he discovered the potato there before anyone grew them in England). He also brought her back fags, which were socially acceptable at the time. I've known men who are too lazy to go to the Tesco Express at the end of the road and get me a pint of milk, so fair play to Lizzy.

The point is, these women and others like them were the first documented divas and in their different ways, they changed the world. They probably didn't even know they were divas, because the word didn't exist in the English language until the nineteenth century (yep, I looked it up on Wiki – it means a female goddess in Italian. The male version is 'divo', like in Il Divo, the hot opera singers).

What is a diva?

So what exactly is a diva and how do you become one? Firstly, to be a diva, you have to understand what a diva is because basically we are very misunderstood, and it is important for me and for other divas to put the record straight. You see, some people have this weird idea that being a diva is a bad thing – fools. They use the term as a criticism. To be honest, it's mainly men who can't handle empowered women who do this. They throw around the term using it as an insult because they are scared and threatened by women who are blessed with diva traits. A diva isn't scary or threatening, she just knows what she wants and she knows what she likes. She is also fiercely stylish and full of confidence. Some people find this cocktail of glitz and balls too hard to handle.

A while ago I did a TV show called *Celebs Go Dating*. You may have seen it. A group of single celebrities were picked to go on dates with members of the public. It was a good idea for a series though I was dubious that it would ever lead to any successful long-term relationships. I feel like celebs and non-celebs are like extra virgin olive oil and balsamic. You can mix it for a while and it works, but after time they always separate. Anyway, the celebs on the show got dating advice from a couple of relationship experts and then we all got set up on our dates. I'll be honest with you, I don't really need dating advice, I've got first-hand experience, but the show sounded like a laugh and I gave it a go. I was so into it that I thought I'd make a proper effort on the first date they sent me on. It was with a bloke called Terry. He was good-looking enough, but he just wasn't my type. I went along anyway because a) I believe in taking opportunities when they are presented to me, and b) because I didn't have any other plans on that particular night. 'Who knows?' I said to myself. 'Terry could be the man of my dreams.'

Now, what you have to remember is that my diva life is manic and prior to the date I had a photoshoot with a newspaper, which meant I was running late. No one's fault; these things happen. Anyways, I always make the effort, so I still made sure I was date-ready and looking stunning for him. I rushed home, did my hair lovely, swept to the side and curled, did my make-up, bronzed myself and picked out a killer outfit. I wore a gorgeous black dress with sparkly sequins and beads sewn onto it. It had a plunging neckline and was split to just above the knee. There was enough on display to whet the appetite and get the imagination going, but not too much. I was like a birthday present where the corner of the wrapping paper had come loose. There was a tiny glimpse of what's underneath, but not enough to give the surprise away, so you are desperate to rip the rest off and find out. I looked classy and elegant, which is what a diva should aim for on a night out.

When I turned up – a mere thirty minutes late – Terry wasn't very happy and he sure wasn't hiding it. I really did do my best to ease the situation, which was a little tense. I apologised for being late and I fronted it out and was polite for a while, making conversation and trying to do my best flirty eyes at him, but I got the impression he was playing games and eventually I thought: 'You know what, I ain't having it.' The final straw came when he called me a diva. Now I know this is counter-intuitive to the whole idea of this book, as I always maintain being a diva is a good thing, but what riled me then was that it seemed as if Terry meant it as an insult. He tried to use my fabulousness against me. It had taken me ages to make sure I looked the part for our date, and he had the hump because I turned up looking on-point. I bailed. I did it as nicely as I could though, of course, because that's what divas do. 'You know what, honey, see you later. Take care,' I told him. I could have given him both barrels, but sometimes it is what you don't say that has the impact. Of course, that's one of my goals in life: to entertain people. So I wasn't too disappointed that things didn't work out between Terry and me. I'm a very intuitive person and I knew we weren't destined to be the Elizabeth Taylor and Richard Burton of Brentwood when I first saw him.

Terry was correct. I am a diva and I'm proud to be a diva. But not in the context he meant it. He was basically implying I was being la-dee-da for making him wait (it's a diva's prerogative to make men wait, by the way).

So for Terry and anyone else who is confused, here's what a modern-day diva is:

★ She's a strong woman who knows what she really wants in life and accepts nothing less. Too many people go through life half-happy, agreeing to things they don't want to do. They settle for things and say: 'OK, I won't cause any upset, I'll keep my mouth shut.' A diva only settles for what she wants; she don't compromise. If someone asks a diva: 'Do you like your cup of tea?', a diva will be honest and, if she doesn't like her cup of tea she will say: 'No, I don't like my cup of tea, please make me another one.'

★ A diva has a backbone.

★ A diva speaks her mind.

★ A diva has opinions.

★ A diva knows what she likes, and the things she likes are often pink and are always fabulous. Sequins are a plus.

★ A diva is assertive.

★ A diva will not be pushed around.

★ A diva has the strength and will to get what she wants from life.

For all these reasons, when anyone else apart from Terry calls me a diva, I am never offended. It empowers me.

Being a diva is about waking up in the morning, throwing back your freshly-laundered 600-thread Egyptian cotton sheets, looking in that big full-length mirror, breathing in the intoxicating whiff of your own self-worth and saying: 'I'm going to be absolutely fucking wonderful today . . . again.' It's a confidence thing.

So, why do so many people think being a diva is a negative term? The dictionary doesn't help. It says a diva is either 'a famous female singer of popular music' or 'a self-important person who is temperamental and difficult to please'. Attitudes are slowly changing, however. Pop music has helped. We've had En Vogue and their album *Funky Divas*, the VH1 Divas concert and Beyoncé's song 'Diva'. All have helped to dispel the myth that a diva is a pain in the arse. If being strong, assertive and knowing what you want in life and how to get it is a bad thing, then I'm guilty and you can throw me in a cell with Lady Gaga and Nicki Minaj. But I don't think it is. I think it's time someone (me) redefined 'diva' for the modern world and the modern woman. We should embrace our inner divas – diva is the way forward, ladies! As the Spice Girls said (sort of), diva forever!

What a diva definitely shouldn't be

Let's get one thing straight here: being a diva is never about being rude. I am not rude – never have been – but people assume I am because I speak my mind and I speak up for what

I feel is right. I am forward and I put my point across but I do it with a bit of decorum – which is a diva skill.

Every now and then I get a bit emotional, and that comes through, but it is not me being offensive. If I go to a restaurant and the broccoli is too soggy, or the LP Rosé (Laurent-Perrier Cuvée Rosé Brut champagne to give its full title) isn't cold enough, I would never make a scene or humiliate the waiter. That's not what being a diva is about. It's not about throwing your toys out of the pram as a diva doesn't have to make a scene. But that said, I wouldn't put up with soggy broccoli or warm bubbles either. I'd have a quiet word and say: 'Can you sort this out please? It is not the standard I expect.' That is the way of the diva. Obviously, you have to adjust your expectations to suit the venue. If I'm in Maccy Ds, I would probably be a bit more forgiving if the apple pie wasn't as hot as it should be (molten metal hot), but still I wouldn't settle for substandard. A diva expects, and a diva deserves, the best of what the situation has to offer.

To put it plainly, being a diva isn't about yelling: 'I need crystal-encrusted lashes, and I need them now!' when you walk in a room. That's being a knobhead; let's not confuse the two. Do you see what I'm saying? A diva for some reason is associated with people who are rude and demanding. No! They are bad-mannered, foul-mouthed individuals. I ain't got time for them and neither have you. Divas should be celebrated; rude people with no manners should be ignored.

A diva demands the best but isn't necessarily demanding. I know that sounds confusing, but let me give you an example. Sometimes, when I do personal appearances and television panel shows, I get asked what I want before I go on. It's called a rider. Most people assume a diva will make outrageous demands – and some do. Here are some famous ones:

★ Cher: a separate wig room for all her hair pieces. A girl can never have too many options when it comes to hair styling. I don't think it's too much to ask to have your own salon.

★ Christina Aguilera: hot drinks not to fall below 175 degrees Fahrenheit. Vitamin C tablets shaped like characters from *The Flintstones*. Yabba-dabba do!

★ J Lo: white curtains, white furniture, white flowers, white candles and white linen sheets. Pity the poor person who walks mud into J Lo's dressing room.

★ Britney Spears: a framed photograph of Princess Diana. Because the Queen of Hearts was the queen of divas too.

★ Mariah Carey: kittens, bendy straws and two air purifiers. Sounds like the inside of the weirdest fetish club in Amsterdam.

* David Hasselhof: a life-sized cut-out of himself. To punch, maybe?
* Lady Gaga: a mannequin with pink pubic hair, posters of Queen and peanut butter. The inside of the second weirdest fetish club in Amsterdam.

You might be surprised to know that I don't make excessive demands in my riders. If I go on a show and I'm asked what I want in my dressing room, I ask for Minstrels and Evian water (I'm not a fan of tap water. If I have to drink it, I'll mix it with a bit of cordial). If I was in full-on diva mode I might ask for LP Rosé, but even that isn't excessive compared to what some people request. That's as rock and roll as I get. I don't demand that my dressing room is painted pink and that no one looks me directly in the eye, or that I have a bowl of Revels with all the coffee ones removed (although that would be perfectly acceptable because no one likes the coffee ones). When I want to be, I am actually a really normal person too. I go in the pound shop. I love a two-for-one on a hair conditioner in Sainsbury's. Everywhere I go I ask for discounts. The more money I've got, the more I want a bargain.

The point is, a diva expects quality, but she doesn't make outrageous demands.

A modern-day diva is also someone who doesn't take herself too seriously. You have to be able to laugh at yourself, trust me.

You should enjoy being a diva. Harness your inner diva and have a laugh with her. Imagine she's the BFF you always wanted, who gets you the best seats, jumps the queue at the club, gives the best fashion advice, provides the best gossip and gets the blokes buzzing around her like bees to the honeypot.

A diva isn't snobby either. She doesn't look down her nose at anyone or think she is better than anyone, even though she quite obviously is above average. She'll go in Greggs if she has too, but she'll make sure she gets the freshest steak bake and will probably blag a free cappuccino too. She doesn't moan, she doesn't stoop before anyone, she rolls her sleeves up when she has to and she strides through life on killer heels with all the grace and finesse of Hollywood star, leaving a trail of glittering radiance in her wake, like a comet made of rhinestones.

Why should you be a diva?

If we're honest with each other, normal life can get boring, can't it? You get up, you sort out your kids if you've got them, you do the school run, you go to work, you do the shopping, you do the housework, make the dinner, repeat until fade. Nothing wrong with that at all, but how many people wish there was just a little bit more to life? A little bit of excitement and glamour? Pretty much everyone at some stage, unless you are already a diva.

The thing about being a modern-day diva is that you can still live a regular life with regular routines, but when you adopt diva ways, you add an extra dimension. All that normality gets a bit of glitter sprinkled on it, like when Cadbury's takes a normal Mini Egg and paints edible gold on it.

Anyone can be a diva. You don't have to have money or a fabulous wardrobe and a glamorous showbiz life – although that definitely helps. Modern-day divahood is a state of mind and I want to encourage young girls, bored housewives, frustrated mothers and older women who live alone in a houseful of cats to take on the challenge. With the right mindset, life doesn't have to be all humdrum repetition, like *Groundhog Day* set in Coventry.

You'll be amazed at the difference a bit of diva magic can make. People (and I'm talking mainly men here) tune in to diva vibes and change the way they behave as a result. For example, a non-diva will go into Nando's, she'll be shown to her seat and have a nice bit of chicken. A diva will have her coat taken from her at the door and her chair will be pulled out for her. People will tune in to her goddess vibes and change their behaviour accordingly. She's like a transmitter sending out diva waves.

She will get the best service and she will never have to worry about complaining because people recognise a diva when she walks in a room and they make sure she gets treated accordingly. A diva has poise and grace. She doesn't even have to speak, she can just do the diva look and people will understand. A diva changes the energy when she walks in the room; she is surrounded by an aura of fabulousness. It is like a rainbow that surrounds her.

When I walk in the room, people stop what they are doing, no word of a lie. Everyone stops what they are doing and looks up. I get noticed and it is not just because I am on the telly. It's because I am a diva (and I wear a lot of hot pink clothes). I love the reactions I get. Sometimes, a fan will come up and ask for a selfie. Often I can tell they are overwhelmed by meeting me and I have to be kind and gentle to them in case they start crying because of the sheer emotional overload of meeting their role model. Other times people will just look. Some men will look for too long and their wife or partner will have to nudge them under the table or tell them to close their gaping mouth. When I enter a space, people know I've arrived, and I don't even have to make a big song and dance about it. That's because I have diva power. It's an electricity that flows from me and through me.

Being a diva means being direct and the best thing about that is all the time it saves you. For example, dating guys can be a massive waste of effort sometimes but it's a necessary evil if you fancy being in a relationship. It takes a couple of dates before you really get the measure of someone because you are both on your best behaviour the first few occasions you meet.

You talk about the music you like or the films you've seen, when what you really want to know is what he takes home after tax, does he own his own house, has he got any pre-existing health conditions, has he got his own teeth, has he got kids, is he on bail for anything and is his ex a psycho who refuses to let him go. No one wants to bankroll a bloke with erectile dysfunction who still lives with his mum.

Sadly, usually it takes about three dates to find out these pertinent details because people pussy-foot around the questions. They are too sensitive. You might ask about his job on the first date, but the salary is probably something you learn months later, by which point you have already invested your time in the relationship. But for a diva, this is not a problem. She'll have a questionnaire ready on the first date and a spreadsheet in which to input the answers. Maybe even a clipboard if you're really lucky. And if the date doesn't measure up, it's time to say hasta la vista baby. A diva will not flinch at cutting a date short if everything's not perfect. She'll do it nicely, with a smile on her face, but ultimately she'll do it quickly and save herself a load of time and hassle.

The list of advantages is endless. You'll look better; you'll feel better about yourself; you'll have some glamour in your life; you will have more shoes and more handbags. You might even find yourself on a reality television show. Once you open yourself to the world of divahood, the possibilities are endless.

Diva goddesses

Marilyn Monroe

MM is the queen diva in my opinion. She's my heroine and my inspiration. I've got photographs of her up in my living room as she is an icon. Some days I feel like I *am* her, reincarnated. I would have loved to have met her. I think we would have had some great girlie nights out and understood each other. I sometimes think I am a modern-day Marilyn: misunderstood, lusted after by men, blonde, curvy. Marilyn had the right mix of vulnerability, determination and steel. She could play the diva role but could also be shy and modest, much like myself.

Madonna

When I was growing up I had Robbie Williams posters all over my wall. I loved Take That – I lived and breathed them. Robbie was my favourite. I wanted to be with him physically. That boy who is now a man ticked all the boxes for me. He was wild, he was dangerous, he was this, he was that. My best mate Vicky was into East 17 and we sometimes nearly came to blows about who was better. Basically, Robbie was my teen crush and my eye candy, but my role model was always Madonna. Not only is she supremely talented and can knock out a tune, she also doesn't give a shit what people think of her and will stop at nothing to get what she wants – whether that happens to be an adopted kid from Malawi or custody of her own son from Guy Ritchie. I've not met her yet but I know one day I will. She'll hear about me and she'll want to hang out with me.

Beyoncé

Like a true diva, Bey will never shy away from speaking her mind. She's happy to write songs slagging off people she doesn't like, she made a whole album devoted to shaming her hubby, Jay-Z, after he cheated on her, and she starred in a music video in which she smashed up shit with a baseball bat – this lady doesn't mess around. She invented bootylicious and dresses from head to toe in designer gear. In nightclubs from Dubai and Marbella to the West End and Romford, every Friday night you'll find thousands of women clutching prosecco minis singing along to Beyoncé's diva anthem, 'Single Ladies' – even the married ones.

Mariah

Mariah is the most misunderstood diva goddess. She once got told by a film production company that they could only afford an economy class seat for her, so she bought every other seat on the flight and travelled alone. She sleeps with twenty humidifiers around her bed to keep her voice in good condition. Her dog flies on a private jet and has a chauffeur. She once arrived ninety minutes late to an awards ceremony because she broke a fingernail. On a junket to London she insisted the hotel she stayed in rolled out a red carpet lined with candles when she arrived. Haters will point to these examples and say she's mad and overindulged. I say she's a woman who knows what she wants out of life.

Dolly Parton

It takes balls to build a theme park devoted to yourself, and that's just what Dolly did. That alone qualifies her as a queen diva. She also travels the world in a tour bus that has a pink master suite, a room for her wigs and a dressing room. She's a no-bullshit businesswoman and has never had to rely on a man. She's got the two most important attributes a diva needs: big hair and curves. How many times have you seen pap pictures of Dolly nipping to the corner shop in a trackie, without full make-up? Never. And that's because an alpha diva will never let her guard down.

Whitney

When Whitney – God rest her soul – was in full diva mode few could touch her. She travelled with an impressive entourage, stayed in the presidential suites and wasn't afraid to let rip at anyone who narked her.

Princess Di

Never cheat on a diva; her revenge will be epic. Prince Charlie discovered this when Princess Di went on TV to tell the world about his affair. She was a class act was Lady Di. She proved that you can be a princess, a fashion icon and a mother all at the same time. And despite her busy schedule jetting around the world, staying in the best hotels, she still found time to clear minefields.

Reach inside yourself and pull out your inner diva

It takes energy to be a diva. You have to get yourself into the right mindset and flick your diva switch. I compare it to having a split personality. The best divas all have their alter egos and the lines between them and their diva personalities often blur. Norma Jean had Marilyn, Beyoncé has Sasha Fierce, I have The GC. I love The GC, I love being her, but she isn't me; I control her and I would never let her take over my life because she'd drive me absolutely fucking nuts. To get into The GC mode I need to psych myself up and when I've been The GC for a day, I need to put her back in her box and lie down in a dark room for a few days.

To be a diva, you need to understand why you want to be a diva in the first place. This involves a lot of thought and introspection, but I'll help you with that and cut to the conclusion, which is that you want to be a diva because being a diva is much better than not being a diva. Obviously not everyone will be a diva because not everyone can be fabulous, but someone has to do it and it may as well be you. And remember: if you are not a diva, you run the risk of being normal. There's nothing wrong with being normal, but being a diva is better.

Some people are lucky enough to be born divas. They grow up in situations where the only possible outcome is that they'll be divas. They'll have mothers who encourage them to be a princess (which was what happened to me), or they'll copy another diva and grow into one themselves – a process I like to call divolution. This is what I'm hoping you will achieve by following my example.

Every woman has the power to awaken the diva within. It helps to have some mantras that you can repeat to yourself in the mirror to get yourself in the mood. Normally, I wouldn't go in for that New Age mumbo jumbo – a diva is a realist. But for diva beginners, a few choice phrases will help the transformation. For example, before a shopping trip, try something like: '*I will have those Louboutins, I will have those Louboutins.*' Or: '*I deserve Louis Vuitton, I deserve Louis Vuitton.*' You don't have to actually buy the stuff, especially if you can't afford it. Just imagining something will help focus your mind on achieving it. It's the same trick sportspeople use before they compete and probably the same trick Kate Middleton used when she realised she'd rocked up at the university where Prince William was studying. Other mantras include: '*I am fabulous, I'm a sassy diva* and *you ain't getting none of this candy,*' which is one of my personal favourites.

It also helps to have goals. Mine are to be a legend in all territories, to inspire everyone I meet, to break the US, to star in a movie with Rebel Wilson and Melissa McCarthy, to live in LA half of the year and a country pile in the UK near Brentwood for the other half, and to get into horses when I'm a bit older. Don't let people tell you that your ambitions are unrealistic, unless you strive to be a unicorn farmer, in which case you probably need help.

Why the world needs divas

Not a lot of people realise that there was a time when I wasn't famous. In fact, fame came late in life for me. I was always destined to be famous but it took fame thirty years to find me. While I was waiting I did some normal jobs, one of which was working in a care home with mentally ill people. I only worked there for a couple of weeks and it was a million miles away from being on *TOWIE*, but it was just as rewarding, if not more so. I became very attached to the patients who were there. I helped out with all aspects of their day-to-day care. I got them dressed, helped them eat and assisted them on days out. I enjoyed it and it felt good doing something worthwhile. The people in the home were there for a number of reasons. Some had been in accidents, some had illnesses that affected them mentally, some had suffered strokes.

What's all this got to do with divas, you are asking. The point is, life is short and everything can change in the blink of an eye, like it did for those people. Life can be cruel, it can be hard and everything can be taken away from you in an instant. Which is why it is your duty to sparkle as much as you can, while you can. Because one day, you might not be able to sparkle, and when that day comes, you'll wish you had. Every girl has a duty to spread diva fabulousness in the world because it makes the world a better place.

And let's face it, the world can be a proper bore sometimes. You've only got to turn on the news to see how glum things are. News should come with a health warning. I turn it on and within a few minutes I'm reaching for the prosecco to take the edge off the negativity. Flick over the channels to a soap instead and things are just as dreary. If there's not a tram crashing into a bingo hall or a Tube carriage derailing onto a corner shop, there's a gas explosion in a pub or a foot and mouth epidemic on a farm. So instead, you reach for a real-life magazine to help you unwind. More flipping doom and gloom. Here's a list of the type of things that happen in real life, according to covers of real-life magazines:

- ★ I was blinded by a sausage
- ★ Docs made me new lips out of my vagina (*obvs not heard about Restylane filler then*)
- ★ I fart on men's faces for money
- ★ I have 50 orgasms a day since I ate pavlova (*I'd call that a win-win*)
- ★ Devil gran danced with hubby's head on a pitchfork
- ★ I can't have sex 'cos of my bingo wings

If this is a true indication of the type of things that happen in real life, there can be no doubt that the world needs divas and it needs divas now.

Faking it

The world is full of fakes: fake news, fake DVDs, fake boobs, Fake Bake. Sometimes it is hard to tell what's real and what's not. It's the same when it comes to divas. Some people will be so desperate to be a diva but they do it all wrong and end up being fake divas. Really, we should sympathise with these poor unfortunate souls; after all, they just want to be wonderful and with the right coaxing and training they can be. One of the main mistakes fake divas make is to confuse divadom with materialism. You should never make money and possessions your ultimate aim because you'll never be satisfied and will end up chasing your tail, and you'll also always be well jel of the people who have more than you. There's an old saying that you can't polish a turd, but you can roll it in glitter and make it look nice. I've never tried and don't intend to, but what I guess it means is that no matter how much you dress something up, if it ain't classy underneath, it never will be classy. Which is why being a diva starts with having the right attitude. You cannot fake it. It starts in your head and heart. Once you have mastered that, you can move on to the shoes and the hair.

When a real diva walks into a room, the atmosphere lights up. She trails rainbows in her wake. When a fake diva walks into a room, it is like someone farted and followed through; people turn their noses up and gag involuntarily. The streets of Essex are full of fake wannabes, tottering around on heels they can't walk in, trying desperately to be noticed. A real diva doesn't have to try to get noticed, she can't help but be noticed. The ultimate goal for most fake divas is to get photographed by a paparazzi and to spend a night in a Travelodge with a

Championship League footballer because that's what they think glamour is all about. These are the things that a real diva will actively try to avoid (I haven't got anything against Travelodges, by the way, I just wouldn't fancy spending a night in one with a footballer unless I was in a committed relationship with him and the nearest Crowne Plaza was fully booked).

A fake diva can often look just like a real diva. The only way to tell the two apart is attitude. To help spot one, I've devised a four-point plan of things to look out for and to avoid, which I call the B-ware plan (this stuff isn't just thrown together, each of the points start with a B – geddit?):

Bitchiness

Real divas believe in the power of sisterhood. We are all girls together, so we should be there for each other and support each other. It doesn't matter what colour you are or what size you are, if you're a real diva you will take everyone on face value and treat them all the same (until they do something to piss you off). A fake diva will make snap judgements based on appearance and slag off other girls behind their backs – even her friends.

Bullying

A fake diva will do her best to put people down and will try to bully others to make herself feel better about her own insecurities. In my opinion, there is nothing worse in life than a bully. I speak from experience here because when I was a schoolkid, I was bullied. I was picked on because of my outgoing nature. It got so bad that I would do anything to get out of going to school. I used to pretend to my mum I was going to lessons, then get on the 296 bus to Ilford where my friend Rachel lived. She'd bunk off too and we'd spend the days making up song and dance routines in her house while her parents were at work. At 2.30 each afternoon I'd go back home and Mum never knew. If I did have to go to school I would get really bad anxiety, which manifested itself in strange ways. I could never go to the toilet and do a number two in the school bogs. I used to get my mum to pick me up and take me home in my lunch hour so I could have a shit. I didn't like the tracing toilet paper there either, so Mum put a double deluxe roll of Andrex in my schoolbag each day, just in case I ever got caught short. The bullying was mainly done by the older girls and even when I got older it carried on when I started going to the local pub. There would be a crowd of girls in there and I would feel them staring at me frostily, muttering things under their breath. Eventually I told my parents everything and I was moved to a private school. It was a tough time but everything happens for a reason and at the new school I met Amy Childs and her cousin Harry Durbridge, who I was on *TOWIE* with years later. Anyway, the point is, bullying sucks, and real divas don't bully.

Bad manners

Manners are important for everyone. They cost nothing. A real diva will always speak her mind, but she'll do it in a firm and courteous manner. She'll never be rude and will only lose her temper when she's threatened or under extreme stress. Even in some of the most extreme situations I've been in, I've always been well mannered. I got a lot of stick when I came out the *Big Brother* house but could hold my head up high because I was never rude. Being a housemate was a laugh, but ultimately, much of the time it was boring and frustrating. It was like being in prison but with better soft furnishings. You have no freedom and under those circumstances anyone would get grumpy now and then. I was also accused of game-playing. Duh! It's a show, it's entertainment, of course I played games. And with it being so boring most of the time, I had to make mischief just to amuse myself. But even when I had disagreements with the other housemates and when they were abusive, I kept my poise. OK, so I may have been a bit rude to Gillian McKeith (sorry Gillian!), but no one is perfect.

Bullshit

Just recently I flew to New York as a guest of Netflix to promote their series *Orange Is the New Black*. It was First Class all the way. I was ushered through the airport, didn't have to queue anywhere, had my own car and driver in NYC and stayed in a suite in the best Manhattan hotel. That is the truth, not bullshit. A real diva doesn't need to bullshit because her life is fabulous and even if she doesn't travel the world in First sipping the finest champagne, she doesn't feel the need to tell people she does, because she's confident in who she is. A fake diva is ultimately insecure and unhappy with her life and will try to paper that over with a thick layer of bullshit.

The basics

Well done. You have taken your first tentative footsteps towards becoming a diva. You have discovered what a diva is, why you should be a diva, what you should avoid and who your diva role models should be (apart from me, obvs). Like that giraffe that was born on *The Secret Life of the Zoo*, you will probably be a bit wobbly at first. Don't worry, because like that giraffe's mother, I'm here to gently nudge you forward as you grow in confidence and explore your new surroundings. Don't expect me to lick the amniotic slime off you, though; we're friends, but we're not that close yet.

Top tips:

★ Be proud to be a diva because being a diva is a good thing.

★ If someone calls you a diva, take it as a compliment. If they mean it as an insult, explain to them why they are wrong. Adopt a diva attitude.

★ Be confident and believe in your own abilities.

★ Manners cost nothing but are worth everything. Recognise the difference between being assertive and being rude. Don't be rude.

★ If you feel it, say it, but say it nicely. Spread joy. Don't be miserable.

★ Be real and be yourself.

Chapter Two

NATURAL-BORN DIVA

How come you've turned out to be such a diva, Gem?' people often ask me. And the answer is simple. Mainly it's the fault of my mum: Joan Collins. She has to take responsibility because she really did dedicate her life to making me a star. She used to tell me every day: 'You are a star, Gemma, you walk like a star and you act like a star.' I was her prodigy. With her as my guiding light when I was growing up, I couldn't have turned out any other way.

When I was about eight, Mum saw an article in a magazine about a make of shoe that the Princesses Eugenie and Beatrice wore and she decided that I was going to have the same shoes. It became her project and she travelled all over London trying to find them. Eventually she made my dad drive half-way across the country to a stockist she found so she could buy me a pair. That anecdote gives you an indication of the ambitions she had for me.

When I was little kid, she signed me up to a dance school in Romford, which is a fairly rough part of East London on the Essex borders. Most of the kids there got their dance leggings from Romford market where you could get three pairs for a tenner. My mum took me to a place called Borovick Fabrics in Soho, which is one of the oldest and most famous theatrical outfitters in the country. Each winter, when it was time to get a new coat for school, I was taken on shopping sprees to the West End. When I first went to school, I was dressed in cashmere and had a leather satchel from a boutique in Covent Garden.

Now I know how all this sounds and I don't want you to get the wrong impression. I wasn't a spoilt princess by any means. When I was growing up we didn't have loads of money at all. My parents didn't have the proverbial pot to pee in when they got married. But what they did have were hopes and aspirations for their family. My mum just wanted the best for me and appreciated the value of quality. I was also encouraged at a very young age to make the most of my appearance. As soon as it was long enough, my hair felt the energising breath of the hairdryer and I've been having blow-dries ever since. You can start to see why I turned out like I did.

I was encouraged to be outgoing and confident and was filled with self-belief. From the age of fourteen, my life became one big diva boot camp. I was enrolled for Saturday classes at the Sylvia Young Theatre School, one of the country's most famous drama schools. Amy Winehouse went there, as did Billie Piper, Dua Lipa and Rita Ora. I was also sent for elocution lessons to a voice coach in South Woodford who tried to teach me how to speak posh. The voice coach lived in a big house and I remember sitting in his front room doing voice exercises and repeating phrases over and over, like 'the rain in Spain stays mainly on the plain' (in later life I learned this was true) and 'around the rugged rocks the ragged robin ran'. I had extra singing lessons, extra dancing lessons, extra acting lessons. I was a diva waiting to happen.

I was also born in exactly the right location. As a family we lived in the suburbs of East London on the Essex borders and, like a magnet, the glitz of Essex drew us over the county line. I hung around with kids who had big houses and when we went out as a family, we went to some of the glamour hotspots of Essex, such as Brentwood and Chigwell. Something in me aspired to that lifestyle, though I knew I would have to work hard for it. You can't grow up where I grew up and not be affected by it. As a young girl, I always wanted and dreamed of the high life. It was always on my doorstep. Essex was just such a glam place. I used to go to restaurants with my mum and dad and see how the older women dressed. They were always in designer gear with big hair. Mum was always glamorous too and done up to the nines so fabulousness has always been in my blood. We celebrate divas in Essex; we are very much women who know what we want in life.

I was destined to be a diva. It was a perfect storm. I was born in the right place at the right time and I had the right mum guiding me.

Meet The JC

I could write a whole book about my mum, Joan – or 'The JC' as I call her – and she'd love it if I did. Deep down she's always wanted me to be famous. She's a law unto herself. I love her to pieces and she's the original diva.

My mum doesn't actually live in reality no more. She's always been a character. A while back, she and my dad sold a bit of property they had and made some money and Dad gave her half, which is totally fair and right, but which I think is absolutely fucking mad because I know Mum and I know that when she's got money, she's dangerous. God help us all if she ever becomes a billionaire. Mum is up Harrods and Selfridges every day; she's pretty much on first name terms with the doorman, it's a joke. Most days she sends me random photos of twenty-bedroom Georgian mansions.

As a family we're happy if she's happy though, because she got ill a while back and we were all very worried about her, as far as we're concerned if she wants to spend the rest of her days shopping, so be it. She has a carer because when she got ill her knees went and she couldn't get around very well. My dad works, running his own shipping business, my brother Russell works with him and has a wife and kids, and when Mum was ill my life was mental too so we got her a carer. But Mum refused to call the woman a carer. She was her 'assistant' and she welcomed her into the family.

The JC does not do half measures. Her illness left her with a few mobility problems, so she needed a wheelchair to help her get around. Rather than get a normal wheelchair, she started Googling photographs of celebrities in wheelchairs to try to find the showbiz mobility aid of choice for the modern diva. She found a photo of Lady Gaga in a Louis Vuitton customised chair and sent it to me. I laughed at first but, true to diva form, she ordered one and is having it shipped over from America.

The other day she rang me and left a voicemail. 'Call me urgently,' she said. I rang her as soon as I got the message.

'Is everything all right, Mum?'

'I've seen some lovely cardigans in Gucci,' she said.

I was puzzled. 'What was urgent?' I asked.

'That was. I just wanted to talk to you about Gucci

cardigans,' she said. Like I said, she lives on a different planet where designer cardigans are a matter of urgency.

She rings me up and messages me all the time. 'Why can't you be classy like Kate Middleton?' she asks. 'Get your nails done like Kate.' No Mum, it's not me. 'Go to America and crack Hollywood,' she says. I'm trying, Mum, I'm waiting for that phone call from Hollywood.

She is quiet but determined, and she is adamant about what she wants in life. Like a real modern-day diva she fixed her goals on a dream and kept at it until she achieved that dream – which, as far as I can see, was to have a famous daughter and shop in Gucci. She met and married my dad when they both had nothing and drove him on to be a success in business. When times were hard, she never complained. She knuckled down and severely restricted her clothing budget, which is never easy for a diva. She always had ambitions for me to be a star, though to understand her motivations, you need to know a little bit about her past.

Mum was abandoned by her birth mother after she was born and was sent to foster parents. Her foster mum died when she was six and one of Mum's first memories is of sitting on a chair while the rest of her foster family decided what to do with her after the death. She was adopted by her foster mum's daughter and her husband who then raised her. When Joan and my dad, Alan, were first married, they had nothing. She didn't have ten pence to her name but she was adamant her kid was going to be a star and wear shoes fit for royalty. She thinks I am the biggest star on the planet and will not be happy until I have global stardom.

You read about these parents who drive their children on to be sports stars, like Serena and Venus Williams' father and Andy Murray's mum. Well, The JC did something very similar with me. But rather than buy me tennis rackets and send me to tennis club, she bought me nice shoes and sent me to the make-up counter in Debenhams.

We were driving along in the car the other day, having a trip out to have a cup of tea and a bit of normal time together, and she said to me: 'I was watching the Kardashians last night – how come they've got that sort of money? I mean, what are you doing? What can you do, Gemma, to get their sort of money?'

I said: 'Well, for one thing, they're Illuminati. Two, they've got Kris Jenner behind them. And three, Kim made a sex tape and became famous, so if you want me to do all that, I'll give it a go, shall I?'

The JC doesn't have illusions of grandeur for herself; she has them for me instead. And for that, I salute her.

Diva junior

For my earliest diva moments, I have to rely on The JC and some of her recollections of the experiences she had raising me. According to her, the efforts she made to ensure I had footwear by royal appointment went unappreciated and when she tried to put me in the round-toed shoes with the pretty buttons on the side, I screamed my head off.

According to The JC, when I was a toddler you only had to say my name and I'd cry. She maintains that I was exhibiting diva behaviour almost from birth. I was an emotional toddler and let the world know when I was unhappy about something. I learned how to get attention by causing a scene and my parents would often pull their hair out, trying to work out what my problem was.

'We never knew why you cried all the time,' Mum explained. 'We thought there was something seriously wrong with you.'

She told me about one time, after a particularly long and loud screaming session, when her and my dad just shut themselves in the kitchen, cuddling each other, crying and muttering: 'Oh my God, what on earth is the problem with this child?' They hid from their crying child because they couldn't handle the tantrums!

I don't remember any of this, of course.

At the age of five, I was a bridesmaid at my cousin's wedding. According to The JC, she and Dad were dreading the day in case I started to show off and tried to upstage the bride. I hate the word precocious, but Mum says I was like a cross between Matilda and Verruca Salt from *Charlie and the Chocolate Factory*. I would cry, stamp my feet and generally show off. My parents never knew when I would go on the turn or what would set me off. I always wanted to be the centre of attention and at the family wedding you can see Mum and Dad on the video, looking nervous, trying to keep me happy. They look like two people carefully handling a hand grenade. Mum is in the background and you can hear her repeatedly saying: 'Good girl, Gemma, good girl,' like a nervous lion tamer, hoping I don't kick off. Even at that young age, however, I knew that sometimes a diva has to stand aside and let someone else shine. The day went without a hitch and I behaved myself.

As an adult, I've always known my own mind and I won't let people push me around or make me do things I don't fancy doing. If you've followed me on TV, you will have seen this again and again. It's why I refused to play games or do tasks on *Celebrity Big Brother*, jump out of the helicopter on *I'm a Celebrity* or date certain men on *Celebs Go Dating*. It's the way I've always been and as far as I am concerned, it's an admirable diva quality. Sometimes a girl just has to dig her heels in and make a stand, which is what happened when I was about ten and had been entered into a dance competition. To make sure I was kitted out in the best gear, The JC took me on another trip to Borovick's and paid £300 to have an outfit made, so I could shine on the stage. The thing is, when we got there – I'm told it was quite a long drive – I just wasn't feeling it. We got to the venue and I decided I didn't want to do it. Mum and Dad tried to gently coax me inside, but I had a tantrum and started crying. Eventually they gave up and we all got back in the car and drove home again. The costume went in the loft, never to be seen again.

The JC has a long list of early diva anecdotes. I also had a weird habit of eating ice cubes. I ate them all the time. I'd open the freezer, empty a tray of ice cubes and crunch away at them. I got obsessed with them and would make sure the freezer was always stocked. Mum started to worry that I was going to ruin my teeth and would gently try to ween me off the habit. But whenever she told me to stop, I had a paddy. She was only trying to help!

While these early memories are a bit sketchy because I was so young, I have very strong memories of one of my earliest outings in full diva mode. In Romford – the main town near where we lived – there was a nightclub called Hollywood's. Every suburban town had its own nightclub and they were all the same: a lot of neon, sticky carpets, dark, smelly. They always had glam names like Cinderella Rockefella, Roxy's, Miami Beach or Tuxedo Junction (where no one ever wore a tuxedo). There are rules nightclub owners must stick to when they name their venues. The more dingey the club, the more glamorous the name has to be. If you plan to build a nightclub on an industrial estate in a rough part of Sunderland, you have to call it something like 'LA Beach Lounge and Country Club'. The opposite is true about the names of the most glamorous clubs. They don't have to grandstand. Privilege, LIV, XS, Pacha, Raffles: all exclusive famous venues with simple one-word names. Another weird rule was that when I was a teenager, the worst suburban clubs always had the strictest dress codes for blokes. If the club was grotty and rough, the door staff would insist that blokes wore smart shoes, trousers (no jeans allowed) and shirts with collars (sometimes men would get away with polo shirts). I'm not sure what all that was about but they probably hoped that if the blokes were wearing their best clothes, they were less likely to fight each other or puke on them.

But anyway, back to Hollywood's in Romford. When I was in my early teens the club started to run an under-eighteens disco, or underage night as I called it. Hollywood's was the place to be seen in Romford and any aspiring Essex diva in the mid-nineties had to go there. It was where you did your diva apprenticeship. Basically, it was where I needed to be, so I sat down with Mum and Dad and begged them to let me go. They agreed, as long as Dad drove me there and picked me up. With the permissions sorted, the next hurdle was the look, and that was where The JC came into her own. My first outing to a club became her project. She rocked me up to the Chanel counter in Debenhams and got me a Chanel makeover. Then it was off to the hair salon behind Miss Selfridge for a proper Essex blow-dry. I got taken out and bought an outfit. I was very slim at the time and got a long black dress which had hot pants built into it so as I walked it split open and wafted out behind me. I got cork wedge shoes from a brand called Rin Tin Tin, which Mum got me from Faith in Miss Selfridge before my blow-dry.

When the time came to make my nightclub debut, anyone watching would have thought I was walking down the red carpet at the BAFTAs. I looked a million dollars and I felt proper grown up. The club was full of teenagers trying to look cool and act like adults, trying to front it out, pretending that we weren't excited about being in a club, when secretly every kid in there had butterflies. I hung out with my mates, swanned around, danced a lot (I wasn't interested in boys at that age). It was fun, but not as fun as the preparations had been. Without realising it, I had learned an important diva lesson thanks to Mum; preparation and attention to detail is everything.

A few years later, The JC's training had obviously paid off because I secured myself a couple of weeks' work experience at *GMTV* and I insisted on having this really expensive pair of shoes from Ravel, which was a high-end high-street shoe shop back in the day. It broke the bank for Mum to get them, but she splashed out because she wanted me to make an impression. I went off on my first day in a smart blouse and killer skirt and blazer, looking like I was going to read the news, rather than make the tea (in my mind I was going to be sitting on the sofa with Eamonn Holmes and Anthea Turner). I put a lot of effort into getting the look right but what I didn't take into account was that new shoes can sometimes pinch and cause blisters. My Ravel loafers rubbed all day, but like a true diva I soldiered on and refused to take them off. I kept my composure until Mum came to meet me and get the train home with me. I hobbled out of the *GMTV* foyer like an extra from the 'Thriller' video, got to the Tube and took the shoes off. I was in agony and my feet were covered in a crust of dried blood and broken skin. I learned an important lesson that day: sometimes you need to suffer to be a diva.

Blooming diva

So, I was born in the right place and the right time with the right parents and showed diva potential from a young age. By the time I left school and started work, I was blooming into a full-throttle diva. I didn't rest on my laurels; I worked hard because divas are not shirkers. I put in the hours and had different jobs. I worked in a gastro-pub, a care home, a recruitment agency, a temp agency and a BMW showroom. I loved being a car saleswoman. It satisfied the wheeler-dealer in me. I didn't seek out the glamour and the glitz; it found me. After I was bullied and moved to private school, my social circle changed. At eighteen I met my first proper boyfriend, Nick. His parents were minted. They lived in a massive mansion with electric gates and a sweeping driveway that led up to the front of the house with its huge double doors. There was land around it and they had stables and horses. That was my first real introduction to proper Essex money. The family even had a speedboat that we used to take out at the weekends.

I did OK at school and college, even though Mum used to say: 'Don't worry about maths, you are going to be famous.' That was probably why I couldn't tell the time until I was about nine years old. Dad would sit with me in the evenings and try to get me to do time puzzles. 'Gemma, you are being lazy,' he would sigh. 'You need to be able to tell the time.' He was right, because at twenty-one I had my first Cartier watch and it would have been a right waste of money if I could not have read the time on the exquisite ivory-coloured face.

My ideas about what being a diva means have changed over time. In my late teens and early twenties, I thought it was all about having the right designer gear and being seen in the right places. To a degree it still is, but there is so much more to being a diva than forking out for the right bag. Diva is a mindset, and you don't need money to have a diva attitude. I didn't know this when I was nineteen, so when I was offered an Abbey National Platinum credit card by some bloke in Debenhams, I snapped it up, believing it was a magic passport to a world of glamour. Within a year I was £14,000 in debt. I had no clue about money management. I racked up debt like I was collecting Nectar Points and spent it on clothes, a holiday and Piz Buin and Lancaster sun cream. I had always been given the best by my parents and I was never taught about budgeting. I lived in a bit of a bubble so when it came to standing on my own two feet, I just thought spending was what you did.

I realised I was in financial difficulty when I started struggling to pay. I balance-transferred to 0 per cent so many times that I ran out of companies to use and started to get stressed and ill with the worry. There's nothing like the black cloud of financial doom to take the gloss off a diva lifestyle. Eventually I told Dad I was having financial problems. He looked at the bills and statements and said he was disgusted with me. 'How has this happened? What have you got to show for it?' he asked. I explained that I'd had a holiday and had lots of clothes and shoes. He was unimpressed.

Bless him, he made me pay it back but every payment I made, he matched. It took me a year to clear the debt. After that I cut back on my spending because I couldn't let my dad down again.

The Cartier I mentioned earlier was bought for me, by the way. After Nick, I had a boyfriend called Dan. By that time, I was earning good money myself. I met Dan at Faces, which is a famous Essex club where footballers used to go. Jamie Redknapp, Teddy Sheringham, Ashley Cole and John Terry were regulars, along with TV personalities and pop stars. For this reason, the club also attracted a lot of glamorous fake divas, all hoping to snare a footballer and that elusive night in the Travelodge. I have never been interested. I couldn't keep up with the fakeness and the way you are expected to look to be with them. It is not me.

Anyway, I was in Faces with a friend and met Dan during a £25-a-head Christmas dinner. Faces was easy to get into if you were glamorous enough and female. If you were a bloke, you either had to be vaguely famous or dressed in smart trousers and a shirt with a collar. It was good back in the day. It was like a West End club outside London, so the cab fare was cheaper. If you were an Essex girl and you got into Faces it was like having Willy Wonka's golden ticket. It was very much the scene to be in.

Dan had a good job and took me to Paris on a business trip. We went to one of his client events and while I was sitting there watching his colleagues eat steak tartare and talk about finance, I happened to look out of the hotel window to a Christian Dior boutique over the road. There was a bag in the window. I had been drinking champagne. I swear I heard it calling my name. I excused myself and went over the road into the shop. Dad had taken out a savings plan for me the day I was born. There was about £3,000 in it. It was probably meant for a house deposit or my first car. Instead I bought the bag with it. It turned out to be a good investment. I still have that bag today and it has probably gone up in value. Sometimes a diva just has to do what a diva has to do!

The basics

So that's the story of how I became a diva and how it was inevitable that I'd end up famous. The good news for you is that even if you didn't have a diva mum steering you towards diva greatness like I did, you can still reach your goal with the correct training. And, if you have kids of your own, you can take steps to ensure that they grow up to be divas too.

Top tips on raising a diva (boy or girl):

★ Get them interested in the performing arts from a young age.

★ Teach them manners.

★ Teach them table manners.

★ Expose them to expensive brands at a young age but make sure they understand the value of quality and that money doesn't grow on trees.

★ Build their self-confidence, but don't spoil them.

★ Love them, but don't blow smoke up their arse.

Chapter Three

DIVA ON THE COUCH:
THE PSYCHOLOGY OF A DIVA
(AND GHOSTS)

Basically, I was born full of diva potential but I needed somewhere to put all that diva-ness. That's where The GC comes in. This is all a bit complicated and a psychologist's wet dream (and to be honest I get confused by it all too). But the basics are that me – Gemma – and The GC are two different people sharing the same body and wardrobe. The GC is someone Gemma Collins turns into when it's time to be the ultimate diva. Does that make sense? It's like Bruce Banner and Hulk, or Beyoncé and her alter ego, Sasha Fierce. When Bey wants to turn it on, she turns into Sasha. In normal life, Bey will not be wandering around the house all sexy and sassy in a crystal-encrusted leotard, belting out nursery rhymes for her kids Blue, Rumi and Sir, twerking in front of Jay-Z while she makes the dinner. As nice as that sounds, I can guarantee that Mr Z would eventually get fed up with it. He would have ninety-nine problems, plus one, because being a full-on diva eventually gets exhausting for everyone involved. Sometimes it's like I'm possessed. I can usually turn The GC on and off, but sometimes she makes an appearance unannounced and I have to put her back in her box, which is an imaginary Fabergé one I keep locked up in the back of my mind.

The GC is an invention. Sometimes I wonder if I've created a monster. She came into being during the second series I was in *TOWIE*. At the time I started to realise that I was going to be really famous because I was getting more and more attention from the producers and increasing airtime on the show. That's how *TOWIE* works. Everyone in it is real and the situations we get into are real. In telly language it is what's called 'scripted reality'.

When the producers realised how hugely popular I was with the viewers I felt as if I had to ramp things up a bit, and that's how I created The GC. I sat there and I thought: 'Fuck, how do I make my life even more dramatic and fabulous?' Gemma was just a sweet home girl who loved her family and had diva tendencies, but they wanted more; they wanted someone who would fit in the *TOWIE* world and turn it on its head. So, I turned up my inner diva dial to maximum and gave them The

GC. Sam Faiers was the first person to call me The GC and the legend was born.

Sometimes the crossover between Gemma and The GC is unnoticeable. Sometimes she'll just come out in an everyday situation, and when she does I usually do an Instagram Live. I could be walking down the high street and the urge to bring out The GC comes on. Usually, though, I have a ritual that I have to do to become The GC. First, I have to go somewhere quiet and have a lie down or an hour's calm. I sort of zone out and clear my head because The GC takes up a lot of space, physically and mentally. If I am doing something like a personal appearance where I know I am going to have to unleash The GC, I arrange the right personnel first. This includes hair and make-up operatives and a stylist who understands The GC formula. While I'm getting into the zone, they will arrive and start quietly setting up their stuff. When I'm in the right place mentally, the hair and make-up transformation starts. We don't really talk because I'm channelling The GC vibe and it's a very sensitive time. It's quite spiritual. Whilst they are creating the big hair and applying the bronzer and make-up that is my GC mask, I will be in an almost meditative state, like a medium channelling someone from the dead, except The GC isn't dead, she's very much alive. At the end of the process, I am transformed.

If I'm honest, I find it exhausting being The GC. It's fun, but sometimes I'd rather be myself. She is explosive, like a big loud bomb full of sparkles and rainbows. Everyone knows when she's in a room. Gemma is shyer, she don't like a fuss. The GC dresses up, rocks up, turns up and shows up. She sprinkles sass around like it's confetti. My close friends and family watch me on TV and think, who is this person? Sometimes I don't even know her myself. But I do know that she's a fucking headcase.

Reem

Basically, it's the little things that matter (apart from the hair, which should always be big). They add up to something bigger than the sum of their parts. Being a diva is about behaving in the right way and paying attention to detail. It's about how you live your life, how you treat people and what you do. Have manners but speak your mind and don't take shit from anyone. Be firm, be fair and be fucking fabulous. And always make sure the price sticker is removed from the soles of your new shoes. I ain't kidding; this is bloody important. If you remember one thing, remember that. I had it drilled into me at a young age and – fingers crossed – I've never been papped with the price tag on my shoes. It's something I live in constant fear of because I am quite scatty and always in a rush.

Another rule: clean knickers every day. Most of you will read that and say: 'Of course, what kind of a girl do you think I am?' But you'd be surprised. You're in a hurry, you haven't done the washing, you're scrambling around and find a pair under the bed. A quick sniff. 'Yeah, they're OK.' No! Unacceptable! It's a slippery, unhygienic slope from there. You cannot be a diva if you haven't got a clean gusset. Clean underwear was another rule drilled into me at an early age. Every morning I hear The JC in the back of my head saying: 'Do not leave the house with dirty knickers on.' As if I would. When I was little I used to ask her why. 'Because if anything happens to you, you don't want dirty underwear on,' she'd explain. It's a lesson I've remembered all my life. As well as my price tag paranoia, I also live in fear of having an accident and being pulled from the wreckage with torn clothes, only for the hunky fireman who has just saved me to look down with horror and say: 'Jesus, love, you could have worn clean undies.'

Divas don't judge. They have opinions about people based on evidence – like scientists. They certainly don't make judgements based on how people look. When I was younger I was slim and beautiful but was never aware of it because I came from a family that never talked about people's looks. We based our opinions on people on their personality, not their appearance or what they had, and that's something I've always tried to maintain.

Don't get me wrong, I always make the best of what I have and will always make an effort, but if I'm out in a bar or club, having a dance, I'm not one of these girls who always has to look in the mirror and admire myself. That's not what a diva does. Even when I was slim, I was never obsessed with how I looked. I didn't think looks were the be-all-and-end-all and I still don't. I've never been one for pretty boys and I like my men on the rough side. For a diva, the most important thing is personality. If people are polite and they make me laugh, I'll get on with them.

A diva is a really positive person who just wants to have fun. There is a misconception that divas are temperamental and get angry easily. I think sometimes people confuse anger with high spirits, like when I've been on TV and people see me shouting at someone. It's just me being spirited and there's nothing wrong with that, don't let anyone tell you otherwise. If you want to speak your mind, speak it loudly and believe in your convictions – but don't actually lose your temper.

Agg

There are quite a few things that aren't important to divas and the following ones are key:

Posing

'Look at my new bag. It cost £75,000 and it's made of tiger ball-sack. Look at my shoes! The straps are made from rainbows.

I drive a spaceship and live on my own private island.' Fuck off, not interested! Posing ain't for me. Never has been. I like nice things, I don't mind splashing out now and again and having a bit of a spree and I appreciate a quality item, but I won't go around rubbing it in people's faces. If you ask, I'll be honest. 'Yes, they are Christian Louboutins and yes, they did cost more than £500.' But I will not advertise the fact. I'm not a show-off. I am more of an entertainer. I'd rather people laugh at me than say: 'She's so beautiful.' All the beauty stuff is superficial bull-shit. As I've got older I've realised that the materialistic stuff in life doesn't matter. When I started in *TOWIE* it was all about who can be the first one to get the Range Rover, the big watch, the big house. But them things come into your life and you realise you are still unfulfilled. You learn that the material things don't matter. There is more to life.

Rudeness

Imagine you are in a restaurant and your knife and fork are a bit dirty. A non-diva will sit there and accept it. She might give the offending cutlery a wipe with a napkin or she might just smile and eat. She would rather get E-coli poisoning than make a scene or complain. She is not alone. British people hate to complain. It's not in our character to make a fuss. There are ways to get what you want, however. A smart diva knows this.

You can make your point without being rude. 'Excuse me [smile sweetly], this cutlery appears to be dirty, please could you get me a clean set?' Easy. What a diva *doesn't* do is this: 'Oi, this fork is minging. Sort it out!' That is rude, and divas can't stand rude people. Manners and etiquette are exceptionally import-ant. If you haven't got any manners, you are not welcome in my circle and you will never be a diva. My parents taught me man-ners, and even now, if I speak rudely or don't pronounce my words properly my dad will tell me off. When we eat as a fam-ily, we're all expected to sit at the table with our arms tucked in and not talk with our mouths full. If I'm on a date, I'll look at my date's manners and I wouldn't be with anyone who doesn't behave nicely. A bit of class goes a long way.

Blokes who make assumptions

Years ago, when I first started getting interested in men, I was on an early date with a bloke and he dropped me back home after a meal. He invited himself up for coffee. He must be des-perate for a cup of Nescafé, I thought to myself. Why didn't he have a cappuccino in the restaurant? I shrugged and made him a cup of Gold Blend. He drank it and slunk off. He looked a bit disappointed when he left. I was naïve, you see. It was only later that I learned that when he was saying 'cup of coffee', what he really meant was 'shag'. The point of this little recollection is that blokes have a habit of making assumptions. In modern language if a bloke says he wants to come around your house and watch Netflix and chill, he doesn't want to binge on series one and two of *Ru Paul's Drag Race*, he wants to get into your knickers. And just because we are all girls on a night out, doesn't mean we are interested in you.

Laziness

Divas get out there and do stuff. A diva doesn't sit around waiting for things to happen, she goes out and makes stuff happen. If a diva isn't happy with something in her life, she has the energy and the will to change it. Hate your job? Get a better one. Bored with your fella? Ditch him; you don't need him anyway. Fed up with your soft furnishings? Get yourself down to House of Fraser and get a new throw. A diva does not sit around moaning about stuff she can change, she rolls up her sleeves and changes it. A diva needs purpose. She works hard and plays hard.

Lazy Essex stereotypes

Think of an Essex girl joke.

Q. What does an Essex girl say after having sex?

A. What team do you guys play for?

Q. How do you make an Essex girl's eyes sparkle?
A. Shine a torch in her ear.

I've heard them all. So has every girl in Essex. And guess what. Some of us have GCSEs and manage to maintain relationships, have several children with the same man and hold down careers. Some of us even have degrees and six-figure salaries. Essex girl jokes were funny twenty years ago. They are wearing a bit thin now. Just for the record, I don't know anyone who ever held a bag of chips during sex, let alone dropped them during an orgasm.

Authority

A diva is an authority in her own right, so she does not do as she is told. She doesn't do anything she doesn't want to do. A diva has the willpower and strength to say no. I learned this lesson when I was in *Celebrity Big Brother* and they kept asking me to do tasks I didn't want to do. There was a task called 'Just Go Along With It'. It was quite simple: housemates were told to do stuff, and to earn items they had to do what they were asked to do. What Big Brother failed to understand was that The GC ain't no performing monkey, and she also loves to create a bit of mischief. The thing you have to remember about my time in that show is that my priority was not to the other housemates, it was to you, the viewer. It's a TV game show, so when I went in there my aim was to entertain, which I hope I did. In order to do that, I had to turn The GC up to max, and that was flipping exhausting, which is why I spent quite a bit of time in bed. This was construed as laziness by some of my fellow *Celebrity Big Brother* detainees. It wasn't. Being in the same body as The GC is sometimes like being strapped to an adult-sized excitable toddler who's just been given all the blue Smarties. It drains you.

Anyway, back to 'Just Go Along With It'. First up, I refused to get involved in a work-out routine in the garden and went to sleep instead (like I said, the effort of being The GC is usually followed by a lie-down). Then I refused to spend the day in 'jail', which was a little cell that had been constructed for the housemates. The reason for this was simple. It's called dignity. Divas have loads of it. Plus I get cramp. I'm from Essex and most people from Essex have a natural aversion to confined spaces with bars on the door. So I took stand, stuck by my principles and refused. For my perceived insubordination, housemates had to give up all their beauty products and the hot water and electrical appliances were switched off. People confused my courageous defiance against authority with laziness and weakness. It wasn't. If a diva does not want to do a task in the Big Brother house, she will not.

Hiding your emotions

People think divas are tough, but that's not the case. They feel pain, get upset and get hurt just like everyone else. They are emotional creatures, more so than normal people. When a diva gets upset, her heart is so big, there's no hiding her emotions. Which is why you've probably seen me in tears so many times on TV. It's healthy to be emotional. There's no point keeping it all in. In fact, I'm such an emotional person I have to make an effort to try to be more low-key when I'm not working or being fabulous, but it's hard because I'm not really a low-key kind of person. When I'm out and about minding my own business, I'll keep my head down and my emotions in check because the minute something sets me off, people recognise me. Once I'm recognised people expect a big old drama, when actually all I'm doing is going to Marks's to get some eggs and wholemeal bread for the week.

Lots of things make me cry: people being horrible, films about animals, insects. I get through a lot of mascara.

Psychic powers

Being psychic is not strictly a diva trait, but it is worth mentioning anyway because it's a good conversation point. Basically, it ain't easy been fabulous and it helps to have supernatural powers. A lot of top celebs seem to operate on a higher level and I reckon we must all rely on something more than our day-to-day energy levels because being a star is such hard work. Different celebs have different theories about where they get their star energy from. Gwyneth Paltrow reckons hers comes from raw vegetables and Pilates while Tom Cruise and the rest of the celeb Scientology club reckon they get their energy from alien ghosts. I'm not sure about the alien bit, but I'm on board with the ghost part because I am very much in tune with spiritual stuff. I totally believe that I am psychic. In the old days before telly, they probably would have called me a white witch. I have what is classed as psychic intuition, which means I can tune in to situations and people and know things without being told. In some cases, I can see into the future. Like, for example, I can tell if two people are going to become an item, just by seeing them together.

I'm fascinated by the spirit world and I've seen loads of psychics over the years. They always seem to pick up energies around me and tell me what a strong aura I have. I've heard lots of psychic predictions about my life. Some of them are spot on, some of them not so much. I've been told so many times that I'll meet a man, get married and have a baby, but I'm still waiting for that prediction to come true. One psychic once told me that a man was going to come to my house in a convertible car full of flowers on Valentine's Day and was going pick me up and sweep me off my feet. On her advice I got up all excited, chose an outfit to wear, got made up and waited patiently all day. He never showed. He probably got caught in traffic or had a flat tyre. The disappointment didn't put me off psychics though and I'm still a believer.

I believe that some people are more in tune with the spirit world than others and that the psychic gift is something that gets handed down through families. My mum is very connected to the spirit world and my nan always comes through when I have readings. Me and The JC went to see Sally Morgan when she was doing one of her theatre shows once (she's a famous British psychic). It wasn't part of a TV show or anything, we just fancied going along. Sally picked us out of the crowd because my aunt, who had just died, came through. Everyone in the audience thought it was rigged but it wasn't. It was genuine. Trust one of my dead relatives to make an entrance in front of a crowd!

I've always been aware that I have the gift. I am very at one with the spirits. I am good at reading for other people, but I can't always read for myself. I haven't yet been able to predict the lottery numbers, but I do use my intuition when I'm making decisions about people and things. I have always been aware of spirits and I have always got vibes from things. I could pick up on psychic energy even at a young age. I have never really seen ghosts, but I know when they are around. I get a

feeling, like a sixth sense. Mum is the same; she had premoni-
tions that I was going to be famous from the day I was born.

When I was a little girl I would sit on the top of the stairs in
our old house and hear noises, like whispers. It wasn't anyone
in the house; I knew they came from somewhere else and that
not everyone could hear them. I always had feelings that there
were spirits around me. Mum and Dad were quite spiritual too.
They even used to meditate (at least they said they did; they
might have just been going off into another room to get a bit of
peace and quiet).

I have never been scared by the psychic world. I'm fascinated by it and I find it comforting because it means that when
we kick the bucket, it is not the end. I think the spirit world is
just a natural extension of life but not everyone can sense stuff
from the other side.

There was only one time when I was scared by what you'd
call a spiritual event and that was because I sensed that there
was dark energy at play. It sounds mad, but it was sparked by a
pair of shoes. I was eight years old and I was in Mum's bedroom in the house we lived in at the time in a place called Rise
Park. Mum was in the bathroom next door and I was sitting on
her bed talking to her. I can't remember what we were chatting
about – probably children's TV or something that happened
to me in school that day. Suddenly I felt the hairs on the back
of my neck stand up. It was a really strange and unsettling

feeling. I shivered a bit. I was facing Mum's wardrobe and the door was open. Back then, my parents were not loaded, and Mum didn't have a wardrobe stacked high with shoes. But she had a few boxes neatly put away on the top shelf. Without warning one of them flew across the room. It didn't fall. It was thrown, and it whizzed past my head and missed me by inches. It hit the wall behind me with a thud.

The shock made me sit bolt upright. For a second, I sat there with my mouth open and then I started screaming hysterically. Mum came running out of the bathroom to see what had happened. I was so shocked the words didn't come out and in the end she had to grab me by the shoulders to try to get me to calm down. I don't think she believed me when I eventually calmed down enough to tell her what I'd seen. She probably thought I'd been snooping around in the wardrobe. To this day I have no idea what that particular spirit was trying to communicate. Perhaps it took exception to the shoes Mum had in that box. It was the late eighties so there were some questionable fashion choices being made at the time.

Throughout my life I've experienced flashes of intuition. For example, later in life, when my brother Russell was an adult, he introduced me to his new girlfriend, Dawn, and I knew immediately that she was the girl he would marry. I saw their wedding in my head and I told him straight away:

'Russell, she's the one – you're going to marry her and have a family.' Unfortunately, I seem unable to direct that level of insight inwardly to help me make the right choices when it comes to the men in my life. If I could, I would have saved myself a lot of trouble and heartache over the years.

I've always tried to have an open mind about things. I'm not a conspiracy theorist but I do think there are other levels of things going on that most people don't know about. You can't work in TV for as long as I have without realising that things are not always as they seem. It is very easy to twist the truth and spin stories to suit your own agenda. People do it all the time.

I do believe in life after death. I think you should work hard in life, be nice to people and do your best and in the afterlife you'll be rewarded. I don't go to church on a regular basis – I'm a weddings, christenings and funerals type of girl – but I do believe in life after we cark it, and in my head diva heaven would be a place with pink fluffy clouds and glitter rainbows. It would be a spa where you can spend eternity in a hot tub without your fingertips getting wrinkled. I also think that you live your life many times over and you get reincarnated. If I were to come back as anything, I'd come back as me, obviously. Time and time again. But the only difference would be that the reincarnated me would be able to eat as much as she wanted without putting on weight.

Attitude is important. If you go through life thinking positive thoughts and believing in yourself, nine times out of ten you'll do OK. Positivity is a powerful energy and people react well to it. It spreads. If you walk into a room and you are miserable, you tend to make the people in the room miserable too. Some people drag their bad moods around with them like heavy baggage and infect everyone they meet. Divas are the opposite. Even when they feel like shit, they still stay positive, and that rubs off on the people around them. Life is about making the most of the cards you've been dealt. As the queen diva Marilyn Monroe said: 'Imperfection is beauty, madness is genius and it's better to be absolutely ridiculous than absolutely boring.' She also said: 'It's better to be unhappy alone than unhappy with someone – so far', which sums things up nicely. Be yourself, be confident and be happy, even if you don't feel happy.

The basics

Hopefully, by now you'll realise that a diva is like a Kinder Surprise. The outside bit is lovely but on its own it's just a sweet shell. What makes it really interesting is the surprise inside. And that's what I've covered in this chapter: the inside of a diva mind and the psychological gubbins that makes a diva tick.

Top tips:

★ Being a diva can be mentally demanding, so develop an alter ego.

★ Pay attention to the little things – like labels and clean underwear.

★ Be positive, even when you feel crap.

★ Don't judge people or make snap decisions based on appearance (apart from their shoes).

★ Get out and do things.

★ Stand up for what you believe in.

★ Express yourself.

★ Look for guidance from the spirit world.

Chapter Four

FAME!

The funny thing about fame is that no matter how much you think you are prepared for it, you never really get used to it. I spent most of my early childhood and teenage years preparing to be famous and when it happened, I didn't know what to do with it. It takes years of getting used to and even now I'm still surprised by it. I reckon even megastars like Elton John and Angelina Jolie still have trouble adapting to fame. I understand now why celebrities sometimes seem to act weird and do weird stuff. I totally get it. Once you've been famous for a while you start to develop a 'don't-give-a-fuck attitude', not because you are being an arsehole, but because you just can't measure up to the expectations fame places on you 24/7. I totally get why Elton wears tracksuits all the time, or why you'll see megastars out in their pyjamas looking shit. Some days you just have to say 'fuck it' and take a day off from being fabulous.

When you are famous, everyone (apart from your nearest and dearest) expects you to perform and be on fleek all the time. Even strangers think they know you and have expectations of you and how they want you to act. It's fricking exhausting. Some days people can't get enough of me. They want more and more and more. I said to my manager: 'I can't understand why everyone I meet feels like they own a piece of me,' and he was like: 'You are about to go to another level of fame, Gemma; it's going to increase.' I was like: 'I get that, but it really is hard adjusting to it.' Fame is a game and you have to play the game, but when I first got famous I didn't know the rules and I had to toughen up.

Once you are famous there are a lot of new and exciting things you can do, like play hide and seek with paparazzi photographers (or paps), but also there are a lot of things you can't do. I can walk into a club or restaurant and get a table. But I can't just go away privately with a bloke for a cheeky night no more. A while ago I was seeing a fella. He was a lovely bloke. It was an on and off thing. He was from Romford and wasn't a celebrity or anything. He didn't work in showbiz and was a real down-to-earth gent. I really liked him, and we had a lot in common. I felt normal when I was with him, which was a good thing. He didn't play up to me, he even called me 'Collins', not Gemma or GC, which I liked. On Valentine's Day we went away to a hotel and spa for a couple of nights. It was a spur of the moment thing. In an ideal world I would have gone away, no one would have known anything about it and everything would have been sweet. But because everyone is invested in my life, my quiet, sexy break became national news. Believe me, it feels weird reading about your own movements online a few hours after you've checked in somewhere.

After a while you have to adapt to fame. I try to live as normal a life as possible, but I still have to do things that lead people who don't know about fame to assume I am just being a diva. I'll go to places that I know are more discreet, or when I'm in a hotel I'll eat in a private dining room. I ain't being precious; I'm just trying to protect a bit of privacy. When you see photos of celebs wearing sunglasses indoors and baseball caps with the peaks pulled right down, they're not being arseholes, they just get fed up of being stared at all the time.

Fame changes your life, but it doesn't have to change the person you are. I view being famous as my job and no one should be expected to work 24/7. In my opinion, when I finish work and put the key through the door at the end of the night, I am just the same as everyone else, but more famous. When I go back to Romford – the town where I grew up – I realise how much my life has moved on. I can't go clubbing there now because I get mobbed and walking down any high street can be a challenge when I get recognised.

I go to Romford sometimes just to remind myself where I came from. It keeps me grounded. If you've never been to Romford this story sums it up. A little while ago a man was found in the sewers there. Someone heard him, pulled up a drain cover and there he was. He said he'd been in the sewers for two days, wandering around, trying to find a way out. Some people joked that there isn't much difference between some of the streets in Romford and the sewers that run under them, and that the bloke probably thought he was just walking through the town. That gives an indication of what Romford can be like.

I will still go there though because I haven't changed; I'm still a Romford girl at heart. I'll go there, I'll have pie and mash, I'll enjoy it for a day then I'll go home to Brentwood. That doesn't make me a snob. Every famous person does it, unless you're in *Made in Chelsea*, in which case you're in a pretty decent place to begin with. Some people accuse you of turning your back on your roots but that's crap. Look at Cheryl Tweedy. She grew up in a rough part of Newcastle upon Tyne, lived in a council house and had nothing. Of course she was going to move out the first chance she got and buy a mansion in the home counties. It's the same all the way through the history of fame. Look at the Beatles, always banging on about how brilliant growing up in Liverpool was. And it's a fine city to visit and have a hen night in if that's your thing, but as soon as the Fab Four could, they all moved out. Paul went to Sussex, John went to Manhattan, George went to LA and Ringo went to the island of Sodor. Cilla was the same; she loved Liverpool and often went back, but never to live. Why would you when you've got a mansion in Bucks and a villa in Spain? So, while I love Romford and it has a special place in my heart, I'm not planning on moving there anytime soon. I'd like to give LA a go first.

TOWIE and me

When I first got famous I hadn't been looking for it. I didn't go to castings or do amateur dramatics as an adult. I did karaoke now and then, but I was never hoping there were talent scouts in the pub when I was belting out 'Vogue'. I was a car sales executive and enjoying the job when fame came knocking. I think it was fate. The universe was ready for me and I was ready to be thrust upon the public and the world.

I can't really tell the story of how I became a diva and how The GC was born without telling the story of how I ended up in *TOWIE*. I was working for BMW, in a failing relationship with a bloke called Darren, and getting to the point in my life where I was wondering what the future held. Things had not turned out like I thought they would. There was no dream marriage, no children, everything seemed a bit flat and, at the time, I was feeling depressed. To top it all off, the day before the

TOWIE fairy came calling, I'd slipped down the wooden stairs at home, landed on my arse and cracked my coccyx, so I was doped up on Diclofenac and in pain. *TOWIE* had already started and I knew a few of the people on it. I was in the car with Darren one day when, out of the blue, the phone rang.

'Hello, Gemma, I'm calling from Lime Pictures. We make *TOWIE*. We've heard that you are a bit of a character and we want to meet you,' the voice said.

I cut the phone off because I didn't want to speak in front of Darren. The phone rang again.

'Gemma, sorry we got cut off. It's Lime Pictures. As I said, we've heard you are a bit of a character . . .'

I interrupted.

'I can't really talk at the moment, can I call you back?'

You know that intuition I talked about earlier? I could feel it then. I knew something was happening and that the decision I made after that call would change my life. My heart was in my mouth when I called back, and I had butterflies.

She asked me to tell her a bit about myself and my life. I did and she asked me to go up to the production offices in London to meet a few people. As fate would have it, I had two weeks off work because of my back so I went for the meeting. Falling down and fracturing my coccyx was worth every bit of pain because if I hadn't been off work, my boss probably wouldn't have let me out for an interview.

After the call I told The JC. She was chuffed.

'I said you were destined to be famous. This is your time,' she said. I've never seen her grin so much; she was grinning like a dog we had once called Daz, a little Jack Russell we inherited when someone we knew passed away and we were asked to look after it. That day Daz had come back in my mum's face. I had tea and cake with her and then went back to Darren's that night. I didn't tell him about *TOWIE*. I didn't know how he'd react.

I went up to central London and met with a couple of the producers of the show. They asked me a string of questions. 'What do you do? What face creams do you wear?' It was really random stuff. 'What are your dreams?' I told them I dreamt of finding the love of my life, having two kids and a white Range Rover. They found me highly amusing. They interviewed me for about an hour and a half. 'Where do you work? Who are you going out with?' At the time I didn't bother mentioning Darren because I knew it wasn't going anywhere.

Eventually they brought in a guy who was the executive producer – one of the bosses.

He asked me to define my ideal life.

I said: 'I want a Clive Christian kitchen.' He asked me what a Clive Christian kitchen was.

'You don't know who Clive Christian is? Google it; his perfume is £400,' I said.

He was posh and had probably never met anyone like me before, but we had a bit of banter and when I left the meeting I had a good feeling. Being a car dealer, it wasn't too hard for me to sell myself. I turned to my friend Louise, who I went to the meeting with, and said: 'I think my life is going to change, Lou.' But at the time they gave nothing away. After the meeting Louise and I went to Harrods and sat on the seafood stall and had a celebratory champagne and oysters with salmon, chopped eggs and crème fraiche.

A week or so after the meeting, a crew came to film me to see how I came across on camera. One of the producers sat down with me on the sofa and said: 'Gemma, what we've noticed about you is that through all your bravado there is a vulnerability and that is the side we like and want to tap into.'

There were other meetings with other people too. Eventually they called me in and said: 'We want you to be in the show.' There was no salary, just a small daily appearance fee. I was signing the contract in capital letters. I had no reservations.

Dad came in from work that night and I told him that I'd been offered a part on a television show. He asked how much they were paying me.

'It ain't really about the money, Dad,' I said.

People think once you get on TV you become rich, but the truth of the matter is, TV don't really pay very much, especially at the beginning. You have to prove yourself first, which makes sense. Fame is a job and you can't just walk in and expect to be on the board; you have to work your way up. Luckily, I was an entrepreneur. I knew that if it worked out, *TOWIE* would lead to other opportunities. I wasn't bothered about the income. I had a little bit of money in the bank but not loads. The show looked fun, the people making it were fun and I could see the opportunities.

Dad looked at the contract. He is old-skool and said: 'You are giving up a really good job to be on a TV show that might not go anywhere.'

'This is going to go somewhere for me. All my life has been leading to this. This is my chance,' I told him.

Mum tried to talk him round, but he thought I was mad.

I was only supposed to be on *TOWIE* for seven weeks and I figured at the end of it, if it didn't pan out I would get a market stall in Romford market selling clothes or try to get a job selling cars in the West End.

When I started on *TOWIE* I was an outsider in as much as everyone else knew each other, but I soon made friends. I was so popular with the viewers that they extended my contract and four years later I was still there. *TOWIE* is in my heart, I am very sentimental about it because I have a lot of happy memories and a lot of good has come from it. I don't want to come over all Mother Teresa, but I do feel we have inspired people and changed people's lives through the show. I really do.

Paps and how to handle them

Divas have a complicated relationship with paparazzi photographers. On one level, we need them because publicity and exposure help careers, but on another level, they are a pest. They hang around my house, follow me and, worse, they try to take photos at bad angles to make me look like a minger. It must be the first thing paps are taught in pap school – always go for a low-angle photo or a photo of someone looking rough. The worse they can make you look in a picture, the more they can sell that picture for. And for that reason, you have to be nice to them, otherwise they can make your life hell and they can make you look like shit. Imagine if you looked shit in every photo and selfie you ever appeared in. That's the power paps have. They could take twenty photos and in nineteen you look beautiful, but in one you're squinting. The squinting one will be the shot they try to sell.

The relationship is reciprocal because the clever paps also realise that they need you as much as you need them. The best way to explain the relationship between a female star and the pap is by comparing it to the relationship between a turtle and a little cleaner fish (I saw it on *Blue Planet 2*). The turtle (the celeb) is much bigger and more powerful than the little fishy (the pap). Technically the fish is a pest because it follows the turtle, but it does serve a purpose. It eats dead skin and other parasites off the turtle shell, so within reason, the turtle allows the fish to live off her. Too many fish, however, and the turtle gets the hump and fucks off. It's the same sort of arrangement between a diva and a pap.

When you deal with them, it pays to be polite, but you must always be aware that their prime goal is to make you look shit. A while back there was a trend for pictures of famous women getting out of cars flashing their knickers. As most of you will know, the lower the car, the less chance a woman in a short dress has of making a dignified exit from it. Paps would lay in wait outside clubs, lean down and get the up-skirt shots that mags and newspapers loved. Anyone flashing a bit of knicker was guaranteed some magazine space. One newspaper even went as far as employing a dwarf photographer they named Papararsey Pete, who was just the right height to get the best up-skirt shot. It was a disgusting trend and thankfully things have moved on since then. Celebs have also got smarter and are much more careful when they get out of cars. I mitigated the problem by getting myself a large Mercedes SUV which I climb down from, rather than up out of.

Brentwood High Street, home of my boutique, the Sugar Hut and several other *TOWIE* venues is a pap magnet. There are almost as many celebs per square mile in Brentwood as there are in Hollywood (I'm guessing) so the paps tend to make a beeline for it. You can always spot them. They are always blokes, they always look dishevelled and they have that grey complexion people who spend too much time in cars and service stations develop. I call it pap pallor. They often hang around outside my apartment development too. Sometimes they're polite and you can have a bit of banter with them. I will help the nice ones out and let them take photos. Other times they try and rile you up and are rude and scary, and I have to get the concierge to move them on because it creeps me out when strangers hang around outside my home.

On one occasion I was with my mum, we were minding our own business walking out of a café when a pap jumped out from behind a bush. The intention was to scare us to get a reaction and a photo. In that situation I tore into him. A diva doesn't like to be startled.

The pap top five favourite photos are:

- ★ Eating: No one looks good eating, so it makes a good picture.
- ★ Post gym: particularly if there are sweat patches on your gym clothes.
- ★ Holding hands/cuddling/snogging a man/woman who isn't your partner/husband.
- ★ On a beach, looking bloated or fat with cellulite (preferably eating).
- ★ Looking sad/emotional/stressed, so the mags can use a coverline like 'Gemma's Heartache Breakdown'.

The first time I was papped was surreal and crazy at the same time. I hadn't been on *TOWIE* long and someone stepped out and started banging away with a camera. I won't lie, it was actually fun but I was innocent at the time. Years later and I have learned my lesson. It is no longer fun and no matter how nice the pap is to me, I know that as far as he is concerned all I am to him is purely a money-making machine, and the worse he can make me look, the more money he will make. Rule number one: paps are not your friends. They particularly try and photograph my arse because I'm a curvy girl. Who wants their ass papped?

When you deal with paps, the best thing you can do is be realistic about it and go into the situation with your eyes open. When it comes to photos of me, I am aware that there is going to be a bit of grit out there. I don't expect all the pictures there are of me to be perfectly edited; I'm not a Kardashian. I don't mind a dodgy pap picture of me getting published, but what I do mind is when you scare me or take the piss. I know how to play the game; I should be in PR myself and if it ever washes up for me that's what I'll do. It's a game and I understand the rules.

Fan freakouts

Fans are like fuel for divas. I love them and I couldn't do what I do without them. I get mobbed when I'm out and about and I get thousands and thousands of messages on social media. Mostly, it's lovely that people care enough to want to have a bit of the old GC glitter dust sprinkled on their lives.

Most fans are very well behaved. I can be out and about doing my thing and they understand when I'm working and when I'm not. If I'm doing a PA in a nightclub, they quite rightly expect the full GC experience and they get the selfies and the razzmatazz. If I'm just out being myself, having a cup of coffee with my mates, most people respect that. Some just politely say hello, but sometimes they sit there and stare, which is a bit rude to be honest. However, I do understand because I am a big star and that is what happens to people sometimes when they encounter stars – they freeze, like a deer in the head-lights. Mainly people understand the boundaries. Some people, though, have no idea or filter and they will see me, maybe walking out of a toilet or buying a pack of biscuits in Marks and Spencer and they'll be like: 'WHOAH, FUCK! IT'S GEMMA COLLINS. YEAH! I FUCKING LOVE YOU.' This is definitely not cool. It is nuts and it isn't nice for anyone. At times, when I encounter people like that, I start to question what's happened to my life. It is even worse when they try to touch me. I really ain't Mariah. And I get it all the time. People scream when I walk in the room, or they come right up in my face, which I hate because it makes me very uncomfortable.

A while ago a family member died. We weren't really close, but it was sad nevertheless. I was sitting in the hairdressers after Mum told me, thinking about him and some of the times we'd been together, and this woman walked in. 'All right, chuck,' she shouted. 'I think you're fucking hilarious.' Fair enough, the sentiment was nice and the woman wasn't to know I had recently suffered a bereavement, but I was like: 'What the fuck? Leave me alone!' It put my back up because I wouldn't do that to anyone. Some people get so excited when they see me and they always want The GC. But depending on the situation, I'm usually just minding my own business being me. I'm always nice to fans though, and I'll always have banter with them because when you are famous you have to.

My fanbase is huge. I've got older women, older men, and I have a huge gay following. I am queen of the gays; there is no one that's above me as a gay icon, apart from Marilyn. I'm the next in line down from her. They love me, I don't know why. Maybe it's because I believe everyone should be free to be who they are without fear of abuse. I don't conform, I accept people for who they are, I accept their fabulousness because everyone is fabulous in their own way. You are, I am, we are all fucking fabulous. The world is a cruel place, it can beat you down, so I like to think I give people hope.

I get messages like: 'I love you, you have changed my life, you are an inspiration,' and I am very touched when I read them.

Here are a few of my favourite fan messages:

'Hi Gemma, I'm a huge fan, in the last six years I've transformed myself after a lifetime of obesity, I'm a body coach now, you really inspire me as a person.'

'GC, you give me life when I feel like I've fallen through the stage. I think you are just amazing, you make me smile.'

'I am just a nurse doing what I love, I'm pretty sure you get a lot of these but I'm gonna give it a go all the same. I am not a celeb follower or someone who spends their time sticking their nose in on other humans' lives. Sometimes it's bloody marvellous to see someone be true to themselves. You are a true inspiration to many. More than you think. From a person who has always struggled with their appearance there is nothing more humbling than a beautiful attitude to life.'

Honestly, I get messages like that all the time and it's humbling because while a lot of what I do and say is very tongue-in-cheek and I don't take myself too seriously, I do have a positive impact on people and that's really important. Being a modern-day diva icon is a responsibility. My fans rely on me. I'm waving the flag for the curvy girls and the nonconformists and the women who deserve a bit of glamour. It's a weight to carry on my shoulders and I don't think about it for too long because if I did it would freak me out.

Fans are predominantly a very positive part of my life. Some could do with better manners but mostly they are lovely.

Every now and then, however, I get an iffy one who crosses the line from fan to stalker. I've had a few stalkers, though none that were dangerous like in *The Bodyguard*, thank God. But I've had blokes who will follow me around. I do public appearances in nightclubs and there was one bloke who kept following me all over the country to different venues. He sent me messages saying: 'You are my Whitney Houston.' The guy was weird and wore white gloves. I blocked him on my social media and made my security aware of him.

Should you swerve it?

In the fame game I've been robbed, beaten and sold out so many times. I've got a strong circle of close friends who I've known since I was a kid but even some of my closest friends that I knew since I was fifteen backed off as the fame increased. It happens when people get famous. There was no reason and no falling out, they just see less and less of you. As a result, being famous can be lonely sometimes.

Fame also makes you more careful about who you trust. In my job I meet a lot of people and most of them want to be my friend, which is very nice on the face of it. But I have to always consider that I am very vulnerable. I used to accept everyone and be open and honest about my life, but when you start to see stories in the press based on things you've said in private to people, you start to be a bit more guarded. Now, I am a little more ruthless, not because I want to be, but because I have to be. I am very careful and if someone is being overly friendly – male or female – I have to work out what their intentions are.

There are loads of advantages to being famous though, and I'm not complaining at all. I get to meet incredible people and do amazing things. I get opportunities that I would never have had. I'm hoping that at some point I'll be offered a role in a West End musical. I was born to play Mama Morton in *Chicago*. Actually, scrub that, I'll write and produce a musical about my life. No one would have given that a second thought when I was working as a saleswoman for BMW. But now I'm a famous diva I reckon Andrew Lloyd Webber will be all ears.

Fame has opened so many doors for me. I travel to exotic places and I get given loads of stuff for free, a lot of which I share with my friends. I always feel awkward because often, if a company gives you something, they are hoping for some free product endorsement in exchange – which is a bit cheeky really when I haven't asked for it. I'd rather pay. However, if LPR wants to supply me with a lifetime of free bubbles, I'm willing to talk!

The basics

This is really important. Don't chase fame for the sake of chasing fame. If you love acting or singing or entertaining, great. Follow your dreams and fame will be a by-product. But don't just expect to famous for nothing. Find something you love, work at it and enjoy it. Fame doesn't have to mean being on a TV show. Fame is about the impression you leave on the people you meet, so you can be a nurse, or a teacher or a check-out girl and still be famous within your world. If you take away one thing from this chapter, take that.

Top tips:

★ Find your own famous. Don't chase fame for fame's sake.

★ Fame is a double-edged sword.

★ The paps are your friends and your enemies.

★ Never eat when someone is pointing a camera at you.

★ Make time for your fans.

Chapter Five

ENTOURAGE: MEET TEAM GC

Behind every diva is a valued team of people who prop her up, keep her looking fab and support her both practically and emotionally. A diva needs her team and is nothing without a strong network around her, which includes her friends, family, hair stylist and make-up artist. It is a proper effort for me to do the full GC and I'm not too proud to admit that sometimes I need help. It may be that I need the eye of a stylist to match me a killer outfit, or an extension specialist to sort out my hair, or I might just need to switch off and have some quality time with my girls.

Never underestimate the benefits of having good people around you because you can have all the stuff in the world – nice motor, big house, walk-in wardrobe, Harris Tweed sofa, fridge full of Grey Goose, jet ski in the garage – but none of it means anything if you are Billy-no-mates. Stuff is fine, don't get me wrong, but it is nice to have people to share it with. Here's a little thinking exercise for you. Would you rather go on the most exotic holiday in the Kuoni brochure on your own and not talk to anyone, or go to a holiday camp in Dorset with all your mates? If you pick the first option there's something wrong with you. Get some friends!

I'm not going to lie. My life ain't always a bed of roses. Mainly it's fabulous, but sometimes I get down just like everyone else. I have a cry and a moan. And it's always my friends and family who pick me back up. When you are feeling blue, a handbag isn't going to listen to your problems and stroke your back. I can't imagine what life would be like without a strong circle of mates or a close family. I feel sorry for people who don't have that around them. There have been studies by boffins in white coats to measure just how important friends are – they call them 'positive relationships' because boffins like to call things by longer names to make them sound clever. The results showed that friendship is one of the most important factors in happiness, more so than money and designer stuff. So that proves it scientifically. For a diva to thrive, she needs to surround herself with love.

A diva needs her cheerleaders and her counsellors and people who will tell her when she's acting like a twat.

My family are my hub. My nearest and dearest. I love them all to death. They mean more to me than anything. They are the centre of it all. Not a day goes by when I don't speak to my mum and dad. I'm always on the phone to Mum, and she's constantly texting and WhatsApping me. Then I have my mates who I've known for years, long before *TOWIE* and fame. They love me for who I am and they know the real Gemma. Then I have some close celeb mates too.

A good friend is someone who loves you, never judges you, brings out the best in you, tells you when you are wrong and is open and honest with you. My friends know they can be frank with me and I value their opinions. They can say anything to me and I can say anything to them and no one is offended. My mates will tell me to turn it in if I'm being over the top and that's why they are my best friends. I like people who are upfront and honest with me. I don't do cloak-and-dagger. I don't play games with people and believe that you should be forthright and open, say what you mean, and if you offend someone, apologise but stand by your principles. I am a black-and-white kind of person. Tell me how it is, be honest and if I'm in the wrong I'll dust off my glittery shoulders and say I am sorry. I am certainly not above apologising to people and I don't stew over things or hold grudges.

There are loads of other people in my life who I spend time with and get on with. In my fashion business I have associates and employees. On TV there are directors and producers. Plus I have management and PR and all the things you have to have when you have a career in showbusiness. I like to think that I get on with them all and that I'm easy-going and fun to deal with. Some people would disagree, and find me a little bit too strong-willed and forthright with my views but that's life, hon – I ain't gonna change who I am.

Before I got into showbiz, I would read about other divas and think, 'Why have they got people sorting out their wardrobes and cooking their lunch and walking their dogs?' What kind of a life is that? How can you get to the point where you can't even be arsed to pop down the shops and buy your own cleaning products? But my life has become like that now and I need help all the time. Honestly, every minute of the day is spent doing stuff that is urgent at that particular time. People see me in and out of salons, getting my hair done, doing this and that, and they think I have a life of leisure. I wish! Hair isn't a luxury any more. It's a necessity. If I'm going out and doing a PA or appearing on *Loose Women*, I have to have my roots done. I'd love to do it all myself but I haven't got the time so I rely on a team of experts to make sure The GC can kick ass.

Success is all about people. Without the right people around you, forget it. One wrong person in your team can bring the whole lot crashing down on you. I'm careful about who I let in to the circle of trust because once you get a bit of fame, people have different motives. So I don't have the wrong people around me.

'What about men?' you are asking. Where do they fit in Team GC? To be honest with you, at the moment they don't. I'll put my hands up and admit that in the past, I've made some pretty iffy decisions when it comes to blokes and the way my life is now, I'm not really that bothered. If the right man comes along, great. But I'm not hung up on hunting for him. I love blokes but there's too much else going on in my life and they are not the focus. The GC needs a pretty special man to keep her in the manner to which she is accustomed and actually, I've done all right by myself so far. Basically, any man who joins Team GC as a permanent member of the tribe would have to bring something very special to the mix.

Mum, the original JC

I know I've banged on about my mum before but I can't write about Team GC without devoting some words to The JC herself, because she has been the main person behind my rise to fame and the reason I'm a diva. She's the head honcho. I wouldn't say she was a pushy mum when I was growing up but she was the one who massively encouraged me because she grew up in life without any confidence and she didn't want the same for me. I guess if I try to analyse it, she made sure I had a personality, which is the one thing you need on reality TV to set you apart from the rest. She also encouraged me to develop my confidence and self-belief by sending me to dance classes and acting school. All these things are qualities a diva needs. There's no point being dull in life and fading into the background. The JC made sure I knew how to shine – and as a bonus I also learned some tap and street dance along the way. I can make an impression in a room, and do jazz hands. That's a proper skill set to have in life!

I don't actually know what planet my mother lives on sometimes. It's really interesting to watch her because she always seems to get what she wants, but she does it in a very quiet, determined way. She'll have it in her mind, 'this is what I want', and she won't make a song or dance about it, but will just subtly make it happen. She used to be quite a quiet person but as she's got older she's grown into herself. She was a normal girl and had a very hard upbringing but was full of determination. When she met my dad she was the driving force that made him successful. If it wasn't for her, he wouldn't have had the successful business he has now. The reason he's got that is because of her vision. She never put pressure on him to deliver financially; all she did was drive him to do well for the family. Basically, she's now living a dream life and is nice and comfortable because she's got me and my brother Russell off her hands.

I'm my mum's favourite subject. She likes talking about

me – not always in glowing terms – and she likes to take an interest in what I'm doing. She can be quite harsh and dry, but isn't nasty with it. It's just her way. Like she'll say: 'You look a fucking mess today, Gemma.' I'm like: 'Mum, I know but I've been in hair and make-up for ten days and today I want to wear leggings with holes in and a ripped jumper because I want to slouch around.' She expects me to be stunning all the time. But I guess that's understandable because I was brought up to always look presentable. She taught me the value of a good coat and a good pair of shoes.

She loves to tell the story of how, when she and my dad were setting up their shipping business in the early days, she went without new shoes for two years because all the money that they had went back into the business. She had one pair of Hobbs shoes and she made them last for two years. She polished them every day (she was a polish hoarder; she had boxes full of the stuff).

'Two years, I went without. One pair,' she says. Well, she's made up for it now. She loves shoes almost as much as I do.

She hasn't always had expensive tastes. She didn't drive until I was seven or eight and her first car was a red Ford Escort estate. But as the family business started to do well, she kind of grew into her shopping habit.

Mum taught me to value what I have. She bought me the most beautiful coat when I started school. It was cashmere.

She always said: 'We might not have any money, but you are not going to leave this house without a decent coat on.' She believed that you could tell a lot about someone by the coat and shoes they wear. Those lessons stick because even today when I meet someone for the first time, I'll check out their shoes. I do it subconsciously.

Mum loved London; that's why I have an affinity with it. I have been brought up going there from a young age. Throughout the summer holidays we were there three or four times a week. That woman traipsed me up and down Oxford Street more times than I had hot dinners, not because she was buying loads all the time – she just loved the London life and the buzz of the city.

She is the ultimate diva. She doesn't carry cash. To be honest, I don't know who the fuck this woman thinks she is. I embrace her and celebrate her. She really is the next level diva. She is so not from this world, my mum. She is on planet Zorb most of the time.

The old man

On the opposite end of the spectrum is my dad, Alan. While my mother is the ultimate forthright individual, Dad is very quiet. He's on the ball though and he has to be low-key, because of my mum. You can't get anything past Dad; he watches everything and takes it all in, then evaluates it and comes up with a conclusion. He's methodical and smart. Being between Mum and Dad is like being in the middle of a weird game of tug of war where both sides are as strong as each other. My dad anchors me down, and my mother pushes me up.

Dad has a very good sense of humour. He has this big office, he's done everything and made money and had success but even to this day he says you can have all the money in the world, but if you don't know the value of anything, it's worthless. He has loads of these sayings. He rang me the other day. 'A fool and his money are easily parted,' he said, out of the blue.

'Dad, are you OK? I'm trying to work,' I replied.

'I just wanted to remind you of that quote,' he said. He thinks he's Yoda. I'm thinking: 'Fucking hell man, I'm thirty-seven!'

But, he has got plenty of nous when it comes to money, which is why he deals with all my financials. He's forever telling me to rein in the spending. He doesn't always understand that to be a diva, you have to invest in certain items, such as bags and shoes and Chanel make-up.

When I started in showbiz he sat me down for one of his serious talks and told me: 'Money is a poison, Gemma. Do not get attracted to it and don't become a slave to it.'

I was like: 'Why do you work so bloody hard then?'

'Because I've got a family and I have to look after you,' he explained. In fairness, he is not a material person. He likes a nice polo shirt, but that's about it.

I get my morals from my dad who believes that the most important aspect of anyone is the person they are at the end of the day, not what they have got or what watch they wear. In fairness, Mum is the same and tells me beauty comes from within. They both drilled this message into me during my childhood.

Dad grew up in Dagenham and was really poor. He was so poor that when he was a kid, he used to lick the grease off chip paper just to keep warm. That's what he's always told people anyway, but I think he's going over the top. There is a certain generation of self-made people from the east of London who like to boast about how hard they had it as kids. Everyone my age in Essex has parents who tell poverty stories – we lived in a shoebox, we had one lump of coal and a candle all winter – that type of tale. I'm sure it was hard for people in those days and my dad says when they moved into their first house they couldn't afford heating. I can even remember putting bread on a fork to toast it in front of the gas fire when I was little, but I do suspect that he uses a bit of artistic licence when it comes to some of the more extreme stories.

He likes a bit of mischief does the old man. He is the most conspiracy theory-minded man I've ever met in my life. He will sit there at the dinner table and say something like, 'Is time really real?' And we'll look at him and end up having these mad debates about things like alien life and secret societies. I think he just does it to get people going and to get a reaction.

My bruvva

Russell is my older brother. Sadly, there were no fame plans for him. He managed to get out of the dance classes and the acting and grew up relatively unscathed. I was the experiment, whereas he had a pretty normal upbringing. Growing up we had a typical brother-and-sister relationship. We bickered and argued, I annoyed him, and he wound me up. But underneath it all, there was love.

Russell was the classic older brother. He'd find my weaknesses and prey on them mercilessly. When I was a little girl I was a bit jumpy about things and easy to scare. Russell worked this out early on and one night decided to hide under my bed until the lights went off. He waited for five minutes until I was just drifting off to sleep and then started making low moaning noises. Obviously, I shit myself. He thought it was hilarious and despite my distress and cries of fear so did Mum and Dad. My family are a bunch of jokers and we all appreciate a good wind-up. His prank had a lasting effect because for years after I was afraid of the dark.

We didn't physically fight as kids, we just had rows. When he wound me up, I retaliated. I remember once spraying a whole can of hairspray on his bedroom door because he'd done something. I'm not sure how that was supposed to punish him – it probably caused me more harm than it did him.

When I was older, in my teen years, I started going to the local nightclub with him and his mates – but brothers being brothers, he would always prank me. I remember being in the bagel shop after going to Hollywood's one night. We were with a few friends and ordered up about six bagels. Everyone else got theirs and I was the last to put my order in. As I reached over and got mine I turned around and realised Russell had encouraged them all to do a runner, leaving me to pay the bill. He was cheeky like that. Mum and Dad would have been horrified because they are so straight-laced. Russell is like me; he likes to do a deal and he'll turn a penny and make a profit. I ain't saying we're dodgy, but we do like to duck and dive. Somewhere in our blood there is a wheeler-dealer gene. I don't know where it comes from but if we have an opportunity to make a bit of money, we both get a buzz from it.

Russell left school and went to work with my dad. He left after a couple of weeks, went up the City to try to make it as a trader, lasted two weeks and went back to my dad with his tail between his legs. He went through a phase where he was the young flashy Essex boy living the high life. He used to dabble, buying and selling cars and worked down the market too. One of his first cars was a black Ford Probe. He thought he was the dog's bollocks in it.

He's settled right down, still works with my dad and is married to Dawn, who is lovely. They have two wonderful sons, Kane and Hayden. Russell is really successful now and he's got a lovely house and a great life. We get on really well. The funny thing is, now he's had his own kids we can almost see history repeating itself.

Me and Russell were very different when we were growing up. I was all showbiz and dancing, whereas he was happy just being himself. But I think my constant performing used to wind him up, especially when Mum would encourage it. He used to tell me to shut up and stop singing and dancing all the time. But now one of his sons has the Collins' dance gene and is permanently singing and dancing all the time too. Ironically, Russell loves it and is the first one to encourage it. He has a greater understanding of what it's all about.

Bessies

A diva needs her friends like an Essex girl needs bronzer. I love my mates and when I've had a hard day being a diva, there's nothing better than kicking back and chilling with my girlies. It doesn't really matter to me what we do or where we go, it is the company that makes the night, not the venue. A typical night out starts up with a nice glass of LP Rosé or prosecco at my place or someone else's, and we'll chill and chat, get ready, catch up on some gossip, listen to some music and have a laugh. The drinks will be followed by a fabulous dinner in a good restaurant somewhere. It doesn't have to be a fancy three-course meal. Picky bits like tapas are just as good. After that we'll head out to a nightclub or a bar somewhere, have a dance and, depending on how much has been drunk, we might finish with a cheeky Maccy Ds or a bagel.

If a night out isn't on the cards, we'll make it equally fabulous at home. One of the rules we always have is no phones. We don't ban them – we're not savages – but if you are out with the girls, you can't be glued to your mobile. We are there to enjoy each other, not Candy Crush.

I've got a big circle of friends and a small circle of very close friends who I can trust with my life. My best friend is Vicky and we've known each other since we were little kids. We met in junior school and went to an all-girls' secondary school together. Vicky was like a skinnier Kate Moss back then. I was really tall and at school they called me Big Bird. Vicky's mum took us to school in her Ford Orion, which was a classy car back then. Vicky don't give a shit about the fame, she's not bothered about anything. None of my really close friends get involved in my diva world. They know and love Gemma; I think they probably merely tolerate The GC, who sometimes comes out of her box when we're out – even though I try to keep her locked away. When I am with my mates we do normal stuff and I feel normal. They keep me grounded, which is a good thing.

I do have some celeb mates too but I'm not hanging around with them 24/7, mainly because we've all got busy lives to lead. I know the comedian Russell Kane well, but I knew him before he was famous because I know his sister.

Jonathan Cheban is a good friend. I met him on *Celebrity Big Brother* and we clicked straight away and helped each other through it. Sometimes I do have to laugh about the situation. It's surreal when you think about it. Kim Kardashian's best friend is my friend in the UK! When he comes over to the UK we meet up and we'll go out for a meal and have a laugh.

These are my top tips on being a BFF:

★ Be there for them through the good times and the bad.
★ Accept each other's differences and celebrate them.
★ Text, message, call. Sometimes life gets in the way and you can't see your mates all the time, but make sure you are always connected.
★ Your wardrobe is their wardrobe.
★ Tell them if they've got something stuck in their teeth/a bogey hanging out their nose/a zit that needs popping.
★ Be honest about their choice of outfit and choice of bloke.

The professionals

A diva has her professionals. They are the team who make sure everything runs smoothly, who make her look fabulous and who protect her and manage her affairs. Most of these are top secret. A diva should never give away the secrets of who does her hair or which make-up artists she uses. But I will say that The GC's barnet is the responsibility of more than one person. I treat the details of my hair team like KFC treats the recipe for its eleven herbs and spices. It's a trade secret and I wouldn't give it away, even under torture. You could pull my fingernails out before I'd tell you what brand of hairspray I use, or who does my manicures.

I will give one secret away, however. I have a stylist called Lucas who knows exactly how to create The GC look. He's a style genius and he will come around and sort outfits out for me. I'll phone him and say: 'PA tonight, Kent,' and he'll pick the perfect outfit. Or: 'Marbs, two weeks, May,' and he'll come and pack for me. I trust his judgement so much that I'll just let him get on with it.

And when I go to nightclubs I have a bodyguard with me called Sid. I never used to need one, but I get mobbed so often I need someone to keep an eye on me. Sid started as my driver. In the beginning I drove myself but usually I've got so much to do I don't have the time, whereas with a driver I can sit in the car and work. Plus, when I rock up to a PA, I want the crowd to get the full GC experience, so I have to arrive fresh and relaxed.

Sid started off simply driving me and coming into the venues. But when he saw how mobbed I got, with frantic crowds crushing me, he told me that he was trained in close protection and that I probably needed security. I trust Sid so I hired him. That was four years ago. He was right, because since then the crowds have got bigger and bigger. The last time I turned up at a nightclub there was a crowd crush and I needed Sid and seven bouncers from the venue to form a protective circle around me. It was really scary, but I have to accept that it comes as part of the job. It's like Beatlemania. There are people screaming and trying to grab me. I don't blame them; they just want a bit of my diva glitter to rub off on them. I think the fact that a lot of them have had a few drinks also escalates their enthusiasm.

When I get mobbed Sid makes sure that at all times I am by an exit door, so we can leave early if things get too excitable. When we walk into a venue he changes, he gets proper serious, his eyes are everywhere, checking for threats and escape routes. His job is to make sure I don't have to worry, and he does it well. Me and Sid know each other so well I can just fix him with a look and he knows what I am thinking. He knows the look that says 'get me the fuck out of here'. Obviously, I have to be polite to people, but I can give him that 'bail' look and he'll whisk me away within minutes like my knight in shining armour. Sid would die for me; he'd take a bullet or a knife for me, maybe even both.

The basics

As you can see, the job of being a diva is too big for one person. The diva is the figurehead and the driving force, but she can only be a diva with the right team around her. Madge doesn't rock up on her own, she trails an entourage of flunkies in her wake. You don't need that level of maintenance and neither do I, but it's important to surround yourself with people you can trust and rely on and who you love.

Top tips:

★ Your family are your most important allies, followed closely by your friends (unless you have the sort of family that ends up on *Jeremy Kyle*, in which case the reverse is true).

★ Listen to the people you trust but be careful who you trust.

★ Make time for people who you value.

★ Stay in touch, even if you can't always be there in person.

★ Good hairdressers are like gold dust. When you find one, guard him or her jealously.

Chapter Six

I PINK, THEREFORE I AM

The right look is the hallmark of a good diva. The most important rule of all is that you can never be too glamorous, but don't be trashy. The look needs to be fabulous without being comical; it needs to be out there, over the top and edgy, while remaining sexy and classy. It's an enigma and a combination of many different elements. A diva creates herself by her attitude, the way she acts, the way she looks, the clothes she wears, the shoes on her feet and the size of her hair. And it goes even deeper. Diva is a lifestyle, so it's about the house you live in, your soft furnishings, the car you drive, the perfume you wear, the food you eat and even the films you watch. When you become a diva, it's a total commitment. You can't be half a diva. You're in it for the long haul.

Being a diva isn't about dressing like a slapper, though some people get that wrong. It's not about how much flesh you show – but if you are showing flesh, do it with style. I was taught from a young age that making the most of what you have does not mean you need to put it all out on the counter for display. Leave something to the imagination: show some class. When I was a teenager I was never allowed to dress provocatively even though I had the figure for it back then. I was covered up and dressed modestly. I know there's the saying, 'if you've got it, flaunt it', and fair enough if that's your thing, but there is a delicate line. You know you've overstepped it when you hear people call out: 'Put it away, love, no one wants to see what you had for your breakfast!'

If David Attenborough ever did a documentary on divas, he'd discover that our natural habitat is the shops and one of the great natural diva happenings is the shopping spree, particularly when there's a sale on. The mass sale migration happens in the summer and on Boxing Day and on both occasions it's like one of them antelope migrations you see on *Planet Earth*, with thousands of divas flocking to John Lewis on Oxford Street, elbowing each other out of the way to get through Zara's front doors the minute they open.

A diva can turn shopping into an art form. If you ask me, shopping is a highbrow cultural activity like going to a painting gallery. The aim is to look at beautiful things. The only differences between spending half a day in Cheshire Oaks Outlet Village and half a day in the National Gallery is that in Cheshire Oaks, you can take the 'exhibits' home with you. And let's face it, a rack of Kurt Geiger heels is much more interesting that an old oil canvas of a bunch of flowers.

A shopping trip does not always have to involve a purchase, although it is always nice to walk away with something, and you want to try to avoid that empty feeling you sometimes get when you see something you like, talk yourself out of buying it and then regret not having it when you get home (the opposite of buyer's remorse). I like to think of shopping trips as research. I run my own fashion brand and boutique, so I need to see what the competition is doing – although in practice, my fashion line is so fabulous, there is no real competition.

For me, a day at the stores starts with a quick pit stop at Shalom Hot Bagel Bakery in Gants Hill for a bagel. It's a GC custom. Not only is it part of the experience, it is also necessary to get a good carb hit to fuel the hours I'll be putting in on my feet. Shopping is a workout. I can cover many miles in a day. In fact, retail therapy is just that. Shopping centres up and down the country are ideal places to burn calories and get some steps under your belt. The more you shop, the fitter you get. Buy a size 16 in the morning and if you are a really serious shopper, by the end of the day, you'll need to change it for a 14 because you will have burned off so many calories. Honestly, people have measured this stuff:

- ★ Metrocentre, Tyne and Wear. Plaza length: 3.5 miles. Calories burned: 294

- ★ Trafford Centre, Manchester. Plaza length: 3 miles. Calories burned: 252

- ★ Westfield, Stratford. Plaza length: 1.5 miles. Calories burned: 126

- ★ Bluewater, Kent. Plaza length: 2 miles. Calories burned: 168

- ★ Liverpool ONE, Liverpool. Plaza length: 1.75 miles. Calories burned: 147

- ★ Westfield, London. Plaza length: 1.75 miles. Calories burned: 147

- ★ Merry Hill, West Midlands. Plaza length: 1 mile. Calories burned: 84

- ★ Lakeside, Essex. Plaza length: 0.8 miles. Calories burned: 67

You see! If you are serious about shedding pounds, get trudging around the shops. Next time someone tells you to do something beneficial, rather than spend all your time at the shopping centre, show them the figures. You can't argue with science. If you add in the raised heart rate caused by the sight of a bargain and the weight of the bags you carry, it's a full body workout. One word of warning though – stay away from the food court. One plate of fried noodles and a spring roll in the Wok Express can undo a day's hard work on the shop floor.

When I shop I head to the West End of London and my favoured places are Selfridges or Harrods. They hold a lot of lovely memories for me because they are where my mum used to take me when I was a kid. Full-on diva shopping trips often have to spread over several days with a stay in a lovely hotel. I'll make sure the hotel has a spa too, so after a day on my feet, I can get a decent treatment and pedicure to ease away the strain. There's also the obligatory cream tea to have, a nice dinner in the evening and maybe an Andrew Lloyd Webber to round things off.

Perfecting the diva look and lifestyle is an investment. Some people, like me, are lucky and they are born divas. But even if you popped out the womb with a bald head full of diva potential, you still have to learn the essentials. You have to know how to dress, what to look like and how to apply make-up. If you weren't lucky enough to be born a natural diva, you can still become a diva with careful planning and practice. Don't give up and don't be disheartened. Your life will be enriched.

And one final note before I go through the specifics, it's OK to drop the diva look sometimes – in fact it's necessary. The full-on diva garb – the hair, the outfit, the make-up – is like wearing a heavy cloak of sexiness. It's an effort. You can't carry that weight on your shoulders all the time. Mentally it takes a toll and physically it plays havoc with your skin and your hair. Even I get sick of it sometimes. I compare it to Paul O'Grady when he dressed up as Lily Savage. She was his alter ego and he looked great in the costume, but he wouldn't want to wear it all time (I'm using this comparison to make a point – divas shouldn't aim to look like drag artists).

Don't aim to be fabulous 24/7, you are setting yourself an impossible target. It's OK to walk around looking like a tramp now and then. It takes so much effort to look wonderful all the time, so sometimes you just have to let yourself go. Trackie bottoms and hoodies occasionally do not make you a bad person (as long as there's a bit of faux fur somewhere).

Crowning glory

When little old Gemma presses the button and goes into full-on GC mode, she assembles a whole team of specialists. It's like a Marvel movie where all the superheroes come together and combine their powers to do something awesome. When I get together with my hair team, my make-up artist and my stylist we fight to defeat the tyranny of boring fashion. All the parts slot together to create the ultimate diva.

Each person in the team knows their job inside out. They're like a Formula One pit stop crew. Each one has a specific area of expertise – lashes, extensions, tints, outfit, nails. I'm sure you'd love to know who these individuals are but unfortunately, like I said, a diva never tells. I wouldn't divulge the secrets behind my iconic diva style any more than a Michelin-starred chef would give away their family recipes. My look is my brand and my trademark; if the secret formula falls into the wrong hands, every wannabe diva on TV will be trying to muscle in on my team. They must remain nameless and faceless.

However, I realise that you're reading this book because you want to become a diva like me so I'm going to guide you through the basics of the diva look, starting with the first rule of diva hair: straighteners are for weirdos.

I can't stress this enough. If you want your hair straight and flat, you need to seek help. There is something wrong with you. Essex is arguably the birthplace of the diva and within our county in the olden days before double glazing and social media, anyone with straight hair was tried as a witch and sent to Canvey Island. For Essex women, all our lives it's been about the big bouncy blow, so the fact that someone wants to put straighteners in it and slick down that fabulous hair is plain weird. A diva's 'do is her crown and everyone knows that the best queens have the biggest crowns. Diffuser = diva; ceramic plates = weirdo. You need to aim for maximum volume.

Dolly Parton couldn't have put it better when she said: 'If anyone tells you that your hair is too big, get rid of them. You don't need that kind of negativity in your life.' The same applies to anyone who tells you it's a good idea to straighten your hair. When I get given straighteners, which I do occasionally, I take that as an insult.

Even if you are not blessed with lots of hair, or have naturally thin hair, there are things you can do. There are volumising products and, of course, a girl's best friend – extensions. Always go for the best quality you can afford because the expense is worth it and good-quality extensions can always be reused when they come out. If you've had a heavy night on the dancefloor and your tape-ins are starting to drop, a good hair technician will be able to wipe off the prosecco and glitter accumulated from the night before and reapply them. Extensions also give the option of having a range of looks, which is important for a diva because no one wants to look the same every time they go out.

My hair has evolved as I've become more famous; it's increased in volume as my profile has grown. But thanks to wonders of extensions I can also rock different looks to suit my mood. There's the big bleached blonde diva 'do when The

GC is in town, and the more sophisticated Gemma bob, which I use when I want to be low-key. I can't really be The GC with a bob, though, as it wouldn't suit her personality. The GC hair is big, brash and blow-dried, whereas normal Gemma hair is the nice toned-down creamy blonde.

If I've got crap hair, I just can't function properly. I can wear my old cardigan and a pair of leggings with holes in and not worry too much, but if my hair ain't right, I feel naked. It must be something to do with the hair's connections to the brain. I reckon my hair follicles are wired directly into my cortex because when my hair's happy, I'm happy too. Who was that bloke who got all his strength from his hair in the Bible? Samsonite or someone. I'm the female version of him. If you cut off my hair, I wouldn't have my diva powers no more.

The magic of make-up (including the all-essential bronzer)

Basically, kids today have an advantage over old-skool divas like myself. I don't want to sound like an old fart, but if you're fourteen today and you want to learn how to perfect that smoky eye look, you just go on YouTube and find one of the thousands of make-up vloggers who can tell you. Though you need to be careful: some of them know what they are talking about, whereas others don't really know one end of an eye pencil from another.

It's a dangerous state of affairs when anyone with a camera phone and a Wifi hook-up can set themselves up as a make-up expert and start dishing out tips to vulnerable and naïve teens on how to look like Rhianna at the 2018 Grammy after-show party (a look achieved by blending Match Stix Shimmer Skinstick in Chili Mango with bright coral Ridiiic into the cheeks, then mixing Killawatt Freestyle Highlighter in Girl Next Door and Hu\$tla Baby on the high points of her face. Topping off the look with copper gloss on the lips, by the way).

There are some basic rules that all online make-up experts seem to follow. Rule number one: you have to have a made-up name, like Jazzinda DuPont or Flecky Muggeridge. It's all about personal brand, you see. No one is going take Doris Matthews seriously, but if she changes her name to Dorito Mayhem, gets a full sleeve tattoo and puts some platinum toner in her hair, suddenly she's YouTube's greatest Emo makeover princess. Rule number two: you have to give the impression that you live a perfect life and are permanently happy, even if you haven't made a bean from your tutorials and the bailiffs are at the door. Rule number three: several times a month you have to post no make-up selfies, which are filtered and soft lit to provide maximum flatter effect. You do this so people know you are 'authentic' and 'just a normal girl'.

When I was a kid, things were different. We learned about make-up from mums, magazines and the girls on the make-up counters in department stores. You know the ones. They wear white coats, look like they've been dipped in matte paint and eye you beadily as soon as you enter their territory, though they aren't as aggressive as the perfume sellers who lie in wait and hijack you with a squirt of Gucci Bloom when you're not looking. It was every young diva's dream to go to the Chanel counter and have a makeover with one of those girls.

I was a bit of a latecomer when it came to make-up. I was about fourteen when I was given my first department store counter makeover, and it was a coming-of-age experience. I felt proper grown up sitting there having everything applied by a professional. It started a lifelong link with Chanel. My mum used Chanel and I do too. I also wear Chanel No. 5 sometimes because that's what my heroine Marilyn wore too.

I was a late make-up starter because while most of the girls in my age group at school were hanging around Romford High Street on a Saturday, picking out lippy in Boots, I was at Sylvia Young, practising to become a star. I missed out on quite a few years of teenage town centre loitering while I was being trained up for fame. At first it wasn't a problem, but as I got older I started to lose interest in the singing and dancing lessons, mainly because I wanted to spend more time with my mates and also because I started to get interested in boys. I had my first boyfriend when I was fifteen. He was called Lee and I met him when I was hanging out with Vicky, who blossomed into a very good-looking girl, really little and petite. She always pulled the boys, but I still wasn't overly interested. She was going out with a guy called Wesley and I ended up meeting his mate, Lee, who asked to take me out. He was very good-looking and was into judo. He had the standard 1990s 'curtain' haircut (centre parting with lank hair draped over each side) that all boys in Essex were required to have at the time. Our first date was at his house for a Chinese takeaway and a film. Mum and Dad consulted and allowed me to go on the condition that we had dinner with his parents and did not go up into his bedroom.

Eventually I knocked acting school on the head. It was getting too much and I wanted to be a normal teenager. I don't regret going because the singing and dancing gave me the foundation I needed for the fame I found in later life. But at the time I just wanted to have some fun. Once I started hanging out with the rest of the Romford teen contingent I soon learned about make-up, and there was no stopping me.

Saturdays were all about getting dressed up and hanging out. Back then, you followed the crowd. Everyone wore Rimmel Earth Star lipstick; if you didn't have it, you faced social exclusion within your peer group. It was like a magic wand that you waved in order to be accepted. Any girl in the school who wanted to be cool had to wear it. The poor unfortunate girls who had parents too strict to allow make-up would beg to use their friends', risking cold sores and other communicable diseases for just one slick of the nude, creamy lipstick. It was like currency and girls used it like prisoners use cigarettes to gain status and friends.

Earth Star was a gateway make-up. Others followed until I discovered one of the most important make-up weapons in a diva's arsenal: bronzer. My No. 7 bronzing balls were like precious fake tan gems that I'd whack on to achieve a golden, healthy glow. Bronzer is the base coat on to which a diva's face should be painted. A healthy glow is the first layer of the diva look. Older divas had to risk themselves in full sunlight and sunbeds, but modern-day divas now have the choice of hundreds of bronzing and fake tan products. To the diva, that stale biscuit spray tan stink smells like pure oxygen.

A brief history of the tan

In the olden days tans were a sign of poverty. Peasants had tans because they spent their days in the open, while rich people stayed indoors and had pasty emo complexions.

According to Google, the tan became fashionable in 1923 after Coco Chanel got sunburned on holiday in the South of France. She was such a fashion icon that everyone decided to follow her. Sunbathing to get a tan became a pastime for rich and famous people.

During World War Two, sunbathing became dangerous because of the bombs, so women painted themselves with tea instead.

In the 1970s the first proper fake tan products were invented. They used a chemical called dihydroxyacetone, which changed the colour of skin. It smelt of biscuits and is still used in many products today.

In the 1980s, sunbeds became popular and many people had them in their homes. Leisure centres also invested in them and for a few pounds you could put on a pair of tiny goggles and sizzle under fluorescent tubes in your local gym. When sunbeds were linked with skin cancer, this practice stopped.

In the 1990s and 2000s, fake tan was still in its development stage – both in terms of shade and application – and early pioneers risked the streaky orange Oompa Loompa look. But they persisted, and eventually more natural products were developed. Nowadays, no self-respecting diva will show flesh that hasn't been bronzed first.

The diva dress code

It wasn't so long ago that curvy divas faced a huge challenge finding the right outfit. The high street shops shy away from bigger sizes and hide them at the back of the store and most designers ignored them altogether. But then The GC arrived, and the fashion world found a saviour. I became a fashion designer because I could see that curves were being ignored and since I started my fashion collection and boutique, I've been told that I am a fashion icon. I'm not lying when I tell you that those big shoulder pads I like to wear are weighed down with the dreams and expectations of thousands of curvy girls who look to me as their fashion inspiration.

My shop isn't just a fashion boutique; it's a dream factory. Diva fashion is all about having the confidence to rock a look you love without caring what other people think. And that's what the Gemma Collins Collection promotes; we pump confidence through the air con system. I'm hands on in my fashion empire and often you'll find me on the shop floor. I get great pleasure seeing the joy on customers' faces when they realise that there are more choices for them than just leggings and over-sized T-shirts. I'm just putting it out there, but if the Queen ever considered awarding a damehood for fashion services to larger ladies, I know a worthy recipient.

My journey to fashion icon started humbly in the East London suburbs in the late nineties and early noughties with Benetton. I'm not sure what was so special about it as it's quite a run-of-the-mill brand, but for some reason my mum dressed me from head to toe in it. Perhaps it was the trendy advertising. Back in the day it was seen as an aspirational brand, I suppose. I had Benetton jumpers and tops and a Benetton tracksuit. But as fashions moved on, I graduated to Naf Naf tracksuits. My favourite was red with the brand name written in big multicoloured letters down the side of each leg. I looked the bollocks, but Mum still held a candle for Benetton and tried to persuade me to switch my allegiances back. Other fashion brands of the time were Kookai, Jane Norman, Morgan and Guess if you were really minted. There was a constant battle between me and Mum because she didn't want me to dress like the crowd and wanted me to look classy, whereas I just wanted to wear what my mates were wearing. We nearly came to blows over a puffer jacket from Romford market, but she never gave in. I always had to be immaculately turned out.

I graduated to high-end fashion in my teens and saved up to buy a Burberry bag, which was the first proper designer piece I ever got and I still have it to this day. I saved up my Saturday job money until I had enough. If I think it's quality, then I'll invest in it because quality pieces are investment pieces. They appreciate with time if you look after them. I must have caught the designer bug after my first bag because it was quickly followed by a quilted black Burberry coat.

One of my favourite going-out outfits from my early teen years was a lovely pair of jeans and a halter-neck top from Oasis with a zip up at the back and red and pink roses on it.

I matched it with some pink Barbie-style heels with a bow on the front.

Being an Essex girl, I was always glam. Once I hit my late teens and early twenties I lived for my make-up and my clothes. Come the weekend, it was all about getting dressed up. Even casual clothes needed planning and effort. That careful consideration has stayed with me. When a diva looks casual, she puts some effort into it. When I put on gym wear, I'm like: 'Someone give me some diamonds and faux fur with this,' because it just doesn't suit me when it's plain. Being the ultimate diva, I make sure I wear faux fur around my hoodie. There must be a bit of bling somewhere, otherwise I feel naked.

One thing you have to remember when you are a diva is that there is no such thing as a fashion mistake. A while ago I wore a shoulder-padded dress to an ITV summer reception and nearly broke the internet. I'm always lastminute.com and hadn't really thought about it. The dress looked lovely on to be fair but the reaction was crazy because people said I looked like an American Football player (more about that later). The point is, I loved the reaction because people were talking about me and I thought it was hilarious. A diva is a fashion pioneer. People laughed at touch screens when they were first invented, and look at them now. A diva sets fashion, she doesn't follow it, and she also has the ability to laugh at herself. Wear what you want to wear with confidence, enjoy being different and don't give a monkey's what anyone else thinks . . . oh, and learn to love pink, because all divas love pink.

Designer vs non-designer

What you need to remember, though, is that the label doesn't define you. You are not a better person because you wear designer and, even though I like some designer gear as much as the next person, I really believe that. I pick up clothes in Sainsbury's all the time. One of my best cardigans is Tu. I love it; I wear it all the time and I feel so happy because I know it only cost me twelve quid. So being a modern-day diva is not about obsessing over designer things. By all means buy them if you can afford them and want them, but don't be a slave to them. A modern-day diva can make something look designer without it being designer – that's the secret.

If the shoe fits . . .

OMG. I love shoes. I was born loving shoes. I could sit there and look at them all day. A girl can never own too many shoes. I've got over 200 pairs at present. That is around the stock level that I like to maintain. Any more than that and it feels excessive because divas are not hoarders. Any less and I worry that I won't have the choice. Don't take that as a level to aim for, though. Not everyone has the space for such a collection. I have two very large shoeboxes in the style of Jimmy Choo and Louboutin which my shoes are piled into and I have more in my dressing room. Most people expect me to have a wardrobe full of heels but there are some in my collection which people would find surprising; I have loafers, Russell and Bromley flats and nice ribbon trainers.

I'll wear some pairs maybe three times before they go because they have to be pristine. I do believe in having clear-outs on a regular basis and when it's time for a cull, I use a combination of Ebay, charity shops and sometimes my staff will put them on Depop really cheap, so my fans can buy them. I only ever use humane culling methods. I never bin them.

Since I had a mishap with a trap door and the cast of *Love Island* at the BBC Teen Awards (more of that later, too), even though I was wearing trainers, I've started wearing more block heels on other occasions which normally require a stiletto, because they offer a bit more stability, but I still admire an amazing stiletto. It's a sad result of the accident and I'm sure once I've built up confidence, I'll be back in more dangerous heels again. But at the moment, block heels are a bit more practical and safer for me when I come up against adverse scenarios. I compare my situation to that of a champion jockey who has had a nasty fall. You don't jump straight back on a thorough-bred; you have to ease yourself back in gently.

Footwear is also important for men. Divas should always check out what a bloke is wearing on his feet for a good indication of what he's like. If he's wearing a nice polished pair of brogues or loafers, he's probably decent. If he's wearing those weird trainers that fit around individual toes like gloves, avoid him. I form opinions on people based on the footwear they are rocking, particularly blokes, and in 90 per cent of cases I am right. They say eyes are the window to the soul. That's crap. Shoes are.

Shoes are so beautiful, I sometimes buy a pair with no intention of wearing them, just so I can look at them. They are pieces of art. You know when you find the right pair of shoes because there is an instant chemistry between you and the shoe. But it goes deeper than just an instant attraction. Sometimes that chemistry is like a sexual lust; you see the shoes, you know they are dangerous and that they will cost you, but you are filled with desire and have to have them, no matter what. Other times you'll like the shoes at the beginning and over time your feelings for them will grow into a tender, respectful love. Then there are the shoes that become like faithful friends: always there, always dependable. Does that sound weird . . . ?

The diva body beautiful

Us girls today get such a hard deal when it comes to what size and shape our bodies are. It's a crime. Too fat. Too thin. Be this. Be that. Do you know what? Just be happy with who you are and try to be healthy. Nothing else matters. And if you can't get to the shape you think you want to be, don't beat yourself up about it. Honestly! There are so many messages about what people should be eating and what they should look like that no one knows any more.

I feel I'm qualified to talk about this stuff because I've been through the size spectrum. I was a skinny teenager, a tall, lean young person and now I'm bigger. I described myself once as the gobby one off the telly who's always on a diet. That is a fairly succinct description.

I've always had a complicated relationship with food. When I was a kid, Mum would bribe me to behave on our shopping trips with ice cream from the Harrods gelato parlour. That was probably where I started to connect food with reward and comfort. If you did something good, you deserved a reward. Everyone does it. 'I've done this today, so I'll treat myself to a cake.' Mum saw food as a treat and used it to treat me. The treat of choice for her generation were sugar sandwiches, so when the money started rolling in the way she treated me was with ice cream.

As I got older, I started to get into fad diets. There were loads of them around and I wouldn't condone them now or encourage anyone to go on them because they are unhealthy. I worked in a recruitment agency for a while with a girl called Alana and we were always on diets. We weren't even fat. We did one called the egg diet. We had black coffee in the morning with two sweeteners and an egg for lunch, then a grapefruit and a celery stick for dinner. The office stank of egg and farts. It was gross. We were obsessed with weight and lost loads on it. In my twenties I got consumed with the idea of being slim because as I got older I became more aware of myself and my body.

These are the weirdest fad diets I've heard about (but do not endorse in any way at all):

★ Grapefruit juice diet. Fine if you like grapefruit juice. The 1,000-calorie-a-day limit might have had more to do with its success than the juice. Side effects: acid reflux.

★ Cabbage soup diet. Supplemented meals with a vile homemade cabbage soup. Side effects: explosive flatulence.

★ Blood type diet. Claimed that people need different nutrition based on their blood types. I'd be blood type custard tart. Side effects: vampires.

★ Baby food diet. Recommended eating fourteen jars of baby food a day, followed by a grown-up meal. Side effects: colic.

★ Lemonade diet. No solid food, salt water in the morning, up to ten glasses of lemon juice, maple syrup and cayenne pepper and a night-time laxative. Supposed to remove toxins and eliminate cravings. Side effects: soiled bedsheets.

★ The tapeworm diet. Wilfully infecting yourself with gut parasites so they eat the food before you digest it. I ain't making this shit up! Side effects: risk of being sectioned/quarantined.

They say that the camera adds around ten pounds to you and maybe it does, but to be honest, when I first got on *TOWIE*, I was never that bothered about it. I was just happy to be on a TV show. When I was in the public eye, people started talking about my weight, but it didn't affect me. The world of celebrity, however, is obsessed with weight and weight loss and one day *Heat* magazine wanted to know whether I'd consider doing a nude photoshoot. I said I'd do it as long as it was a positive piece that shows I am curvy and proud, I told them.

The shoot wasn't as bad as you might think. There was a woman photographer who made me feel comfortable and it was quite a laugh. When the photos were published it felt like the whole world was talking about me. I did an interview which was published alongside the pictures in which I waved the flag for curvy girls everywhere. I explained that no, I wasn't stick thin, but that I wasn't in Maccy Ds every day either and I was happy with who I was. That was the first time I felt properly famous because I was on the front of *Heat* and was being spoken about on national TV.

Any female British celebrity who is over a size 14 will inevitably one day get an offer to do a transformational weight-loss journey, particularly if she's ever been papped looking a bit overweight on a beach. Usually the offers come from a magazine or a company that does weight-loss programme DVDS. Soon after the naked shoot I was offered the chance to go on a six-week intense weight-loss boot camp. The challenge was to go from a size 20 to a size 12. It was hardcore; it was the type of place where instructors shout at you, you have to hike up hills and crawl through mud and at the end of the day, you get a small bowl of lentils and a side salad for your troubles. To a lot of girls, this sounds like heaven. For me, it was hell. I went with my mate Vicky, who's fit and was up for the challenge. We stopped on the way there for a last Twix.

I was weighed when I got there. I was 17 stone 11 lbs and when I stepped off the scales they told me the rules. It was all early morning starts, exercise every day, no going out and only herbal tea. I wanted to break down and cry like a baby on the floor but I'm a diva and we're made of stronger stuff.

To begin with, it wasn't a barrel of laughs. There was a three-mile run or jog before a breakfast of porridge, more exercise, then one carrot or a piece of cucumber with a dollop of hummus. Then more exercise. Then lunch, which would be soup or a small salad. In the afternoon there was the choice of a four-hour walk or more exercise. It was so hard but eventually, after two weeks of utter misery, I started enjoying it. I'll put my hand up and admit that at points I did fall off the wagon. We were allowed home at the weekends and one weekend I had a sneaky curry.

Eventually, after four weeks I had to stop but by then I had lost two and a half stone and got down to a size 14. Was the result worth the effort? For me, probably not, because weight has never bothered me enough to make me miserable. For other girls who genuinely hate the way they look, it works. But I think, like Whitney says, that if you learn to love yourself, that's the greatest love of all.

I can't be stressing about my life anyway because I've been prone to psoriasis in the past which is caused by stress. When I was in my twenties I broke out in weeping blisters on my head. I remember waking up one night and my head was on fire. Later, I was at my desk working in a Mini showroom scratching my head when all of a sudden, I felt wet stuff running down my neck from the sores on my scalp. It was gross. Stress is a fact of life for everyone and being a diva doesn't protect you from it. There are ways of dealing with it, though. Chocolate definitely helps. So do friends and family. It's an old cliché but a problem shared is a problem halved. And when I feel tense I'll lock the front door, run a lovely bath, put in some bubbles and rose petals, turn off the phone, light some candles and have a soak. It works wonders.

Not too long ago I did a TV show called *Sugar Free Farm*. In the show, several celebrities were sent to stay together on a farm where we all gave up sugar. It was interesting. You wouldn't believe how much food has sugar in it. But the people on the show weren't really my cup of tea, apart from Ann Widdecombe who I really liked. I was stuck there for three weeks and did enjoy farm life because there is a bit of me who is a country girl at heart.

Ultimately, here's what I think about fashion, divas and their bodies. Firstly, I don't even think we should be using the phrase 'plus size'; it should be fashion for all. I'm a curvy girl and I believe in enhancing natural beauty. Make the most of what you have. Curvy girls sometimes wear stuff that's too short for them. When it comes to clothes for curvy girls the best advice I can give is go with what you like and don't be afraid to be bold. There are no set rules. People will say you should go for vertical stripes to make yourself look longer, or wear block colours, or whatever. Just follow your own instinct. It's like using the force; if you feel right and if you look in the mirror and like what you see, have the confidence to wear it. Confidence is like another layer of glamour that sits over your clothes. I weave it into the clothes I design. When I design garments, I channel my inner fabulousness. I wouldn't make something too short or unflattering for a bigger girl.

Secondly, be beautiful and don't change who you are. Get your brows done, get waxed, get a lip-liner tattooed on if you must, but I don't believe in putting things in your face or your body that aren't supposed to be there (that applies to putting blokes in your body who aren't supposed to be there too). Be body confident. Look in the mirror every day and remind yourself that your superpower is you. Be yourself and you can't go wrong.

Do I worry about weight? I'd like to lose some but I don't beat myself up. Most days I'll eat healthily but I'm guilty of eating out and enjoying myself too much just like everyone else. If you go to a restaurant and pay good money for a meal, you might as well enjoy it. As you get older you don't want to be told what to do. It's ironic really; the amount of people I know who pay to put things in their body to fill them out – lips, boobs, bum. And then they look at me and say that I should be smaller. Why should I conform to what they think? Why should any of us?

The joy of food

I don't do drugs, but I love a biscuit. That's my thing: food. I'm not addicted to it but put me in an M&S food hall and I find it very hard to walk out empty-handed.

Food isn't just about eating, it's about the setting and who you are with. Divas make the most of any meal. Even if you're having a Pizza Express, you can make it special. Remember that the menu is just a guideline. If you want a Classic topping on a Romano base, don't be afraid to ask. Not sure whether you want a glass of Pinot Grigio or a glass of Chardonnay? Ask to try both. Remember, you are the boss. Change tables if you are not happy and don't tip if the service doesn't merit it.

The most memorable meal I ever ate was in Venice in the Western Excelsior hotel. I'd gone to the Venice Film Festival with Mum and Dad (that's how we rolled – I've never really been normal). We sat down and I ordered the veal and Mum ordered pasta with truffle shavings.

'Very good choice,' the waiter said. 'That's what Catherine and Michael just ordered.'

'Catherine and Michael? Who are they?' I asked. 'Do I know them from back home?'

The bloke shook his head.

'Catherine Zeta-Jones and Michael Douglas,' he said. 'You've just missed them.'

I was younger then and was always a few minutes behind greatness. Now, I've caught it up.

If I'm cooking at home, my signature dishes are roast dinner or seafood linguine. I cook all the time – I love it because it relaxes me and helps me switch off. I did *Masterchef* and enjoyed it. But I'd only do *Bake Off* as a presenter and I'd have to work with Paul Hollywood because he is hot.

Queen of the road

The obvious diva wheels are Range Rover Evoques, but everyone's got one now. I'm big into the environment and saving the planet so I think divas should set an example and start looking at electric and hybrid alternatives. Lexus makes some decent cars. At heart though I'm a Beamer girl; it's in my blood. I've always had a Beamer wrapped around me. I've got a 6 Series at the moment, but I like to change things around. I had Range Rovers for a couple of years. I had the biggest, baddest ones going. I once spent eighty-seven grand on a top-spec one and I thought: 'I can't justify this,' so I got rid.

Home sweet homes

A diva's home environment says a lot about who she is. My lifestyle means I move around quite a bit. The last couple of apartments I've lived in have been in big converted grand old mental homes – read into that what you will. Wherever I've lived, I've always been houseproud. A diva should always care about her surroundings and should leave her mark on wherever she stays. Even if it's a shared room in a house or a one-bed studio flat, you can make your mark. Throws, candles, knick-knacks and tasteful soft furnishing can turn a hovel into a home.

Before I was famous, I lived in a converted barn with a bloke I was with at the time and the house was stunning. In many ways, it was my dream home. Unfortunately it turned out he wasn't my dream man. When you walked in there was a sweeping staircase leading to the bedrooms, and there was a massive kitchen and massive lounge with a real fire. I had a dressing room and my own bathroom. We had a room to sleep in and our own separate rooms to get dressed in. We had a range cooker and the house was in a beautiful area in the country. I looked after the home and loved cleaning it and buying things for it. I was in my mid-twenties and lived like a Stepford wife. I had a lot of responsibility. While all my friends were going on girly holidays, I was more into buying lamps, curtains and going to Ikea. I matured quite quickly.

The point is, your home environment is important. It's where a diva can relax and it's also part of a diva's look and the atmosphere she creates for herself. For instance, I love an expensive Diptyque candle. They retail for about fifty quid, which might sound excessive but I can't do cheap candles – they burn black and stain the walls (though some supermarkets do great ranges which smell exactly the same as some of the expensive brands!). I'll have a tealight, I don't mind them, but a signature home scent to a diva is everything. I don't mind spending on a candle if it's the right kind and the right smell. You can get diffusers and electric candles, but there is something sensual and seductive about having a flame on the go. Smell is one of the most suggestive senses. If The GC was going to launch a diva perfume, it would smell of glamour and crystals.

Eventually, as part of my business empire, I want to go into interiors and start designing homeware. A diva's home has big statement pieces, leopard print and faux fur throws. She always has a throw nearby to rest her body on. She also needs a big bath, because a diva loves to bathe in fresh rose petals, or bubbles if rose petals are not available. In case you haven't gathered yet, a diva loves opulence.

Chillaxing

A diva can't burn the candle at both ends (unless it's a Diptyque), she has to relax and recharge her wonderfulness. Usually, relaxing is done in a spa, or at home in a big bath or on a sofa lying on a leopardskin throw, watching a movie. Anything with Marilyn in is good diva material. Romcoms work just as well. My favourite film of all time is *White Chicks* – it's a hilarious chick flick about two guys who dress up as two blonde girls and go around creating havoc. It makes me laugh every single time. I watch TV when I can, but because I'm on it so much, it can be like a busman's holiday sometimes. I've only ever watched two box sets: *Game of Thrones* and *Sex and the City*.

My guilty pleasure is musical theatre. I love a good show and one day will write, produce and star in *Gemma Collins: The Musical*. Obvs I'll play the lead role, my mum would be played by the other Joan Collins and Arg would be Chris Hemsworth in a prosthetic bodysuit.

The basics

So what have we learned, my young apprentices? The diva look is a composite of many parts that fit together like a jigsaw to create your glittering invincible diva suit of armour. When you drape your individual diva style over your shoulders, place the blow-dried crown of bounciness on you bonce and slick on the bronzed war paint, you are a warrior princess wielding the sword of fabulousness and the shield of glamour. Now fly, my pretties!

Top tips:

★ It's all about the big hair.

★ Throw away your straighteners and never speak of them again.

★ Be bold with your look and choose what you want to wear, not what you think you should wear.

★ Bronzer is a diva's best friend.

★ Be proud of your curves and love yourself.

★ Learn how to spot a good snide and haggle for it.

Chapter Seven

DEAR GC . . .: LOVE AND SEX ADVICE FOR THE MODERN-DAY DIVA

I'm a modern-day day diva, which means I stand on my own two feet and look after myself. I also love men. Some are absolute gods (not all of them). 'This sounds like a contradiction, GC,' I hear you say. 'How can you be fiercely independent and a female icon and role model to a whole generation of girls, while admitting that you crave men? Surely the two cannot go together?' Well, you're wrong. They can, as long as the diva makes the rules and calls the shots and, most importantly, chooses the home furnishings, the holiday destinations and, in some cases, what her man wears (some blokes have no idea what looks good on them).

Don't get me wrong. Relationships are about compromise, to a degree (you may have to go and see a *Fast and Furious* movie occasionally, just to keep the peace), but some things must remain unnegotiable. Let a man near the cushion section or let him book your holiday and before you know it he'll fuck up your interior colour scheme and cart you off on a Ryanair flight to some weird stag destination in Eastern Europe for a long weekend because the beer's only 20p a bottle and it's got a vibrant red-light district.

Men are great for some things, not so much for others. But I love them and I like the male culture. I love a bit of banter and I enjoy being outspoken. My personality is sometimes very forthright, strong and overpowering. Fuck knows why I'm like that. Then there is the other side of me, which is fluffy and pink. Blokes tend to be a bit basic, whereas women have lots of layers and emotions. Blokes are simple and they have basic needs: food, sex, gadgets. Women have more: emotional connection, sexual chemistry, conversation, security, shoes.

Over the years I like to think that I've become a bit of an expert when it comes to men and relationships – not because I've had loads, but because I've been through the mill with all the relationships I've had and come out the other side intact. I've been so naïve in love before. I've seen the world through rose-tinted glasses. I've got myself involved in men and been like: 'Oh, he's really nice,' when all he wanted was selfish gain and a bit of my fame. I have been hurt in every single relationship I've had and it's left me scarred. I've been left wondering how I overcome the fear of being hurt again, thinking I will die if my heart gets crushed one more time. Then I dust myself down and get on with it. Each heartbreak is a learning exercise.

What doesn't help is that there seems to be a national pre-occupation with my love life. Some people are rooting for me and want to see me settle down and find The One, whereas others like to see me lose in love again and again. It is a cross I have to bear.

I've had so many ups and downs in my love life and I'll be honest with you, as I sit here now in 2018, writing this book, I'm not sure where I'll end up on the motorway of love. Currently, I'm kind of at Clacket Lane services. There's a decent selection of goods and services, I'm satisfied with my progress so far but I'm not sure how long I'll be staying. I've been in and out of love with Arg and depending on when you read this, it could be on or off. It's one of those relationships, I'm afraid.

If, however, you are a person from the future and you've downloaded this book into the chip everyone will have on their brains, I may well have already settled down, got hitched, raised a family and carked it. If that's the case, diva from the future, you can skip most of this chapter.

Ironically, I wasn't interested in boys when I was growing up. Basically, they were never on the top of the agenda for me. When my friends were taking their first nervous steps into boys' bedrooms, I was doing tap recitals, totally oblivious to the Lynx-scented world I was missing out on. Boys never came into the equation. Obviously that all changed, but I didn't have sex until I was about eighteen, which in Essex is some kind of a record (I think it might still stand today).

So, I like blokes. They are my weakness. But I'm not ruled by them. Maybe I used to be. Maybe I used to yearn to settle down and have a fairytale ending, but at the moment, while I'm sitting here writing this, I can take or leave them. There are blokes who I see and who come in and out of my life occasionally, but they never hang around, and I never want them to. My life changes so much from week to week that I can't commit long-term. I can be with a bloke and love being in his company, but then if I don't see him for four or five days, I don't give a monkey's. That's how it is. That's probably why the only bloke who will really turn my head is the explosive one who will come into my life and turn it upside down.

In the meantime I have no illusions about what a relationship should be like. I used to, but several let-downs and wasted years later and I have a more realistic view of what a relationship should be, and quite often I think I'll give it a miss for the time being, thank you. Sometimes I have this idea that I want a normal conventional life where I come home from work and my other half is there, and we both sit down and have dinner together and talk about the day we've had before we sit on the sofa, watch a bit of telly and then go to bed and repeat the pattern until one or both of us shuffle off to a care home. Sometimes that sounds like a nice way to spend a life. In my head I play at being in a relationship. But then diva life takes over and I think: 'Fuck that.'

If I'm honest, perhaps I've always gone for the wrong type. I am drawn to bad boys and, like Marilyn Monroe, I have a soft spot for gangsters and powerful geezers. Inevitably it never ends well. Some divas are destined to be losers in love. Look at some of the biggest divas in history like Marilyn and Princess Di. Things didn't work out well for them. I guess it's because the main diva relationship rule is 'never lose your way for a man'. Respect men, enjoy their company but you have to be the woman you are. Some men can't live with that.

My ideal geezers

Liam Neeson

Maybe it's the sexy Irish accent, maybe it's the hulking 6 foot 3 inch body, maybe it's because if I ever got kidnapped I know he'd rescue me and kill all the bad guys, but Liam is one of my celebrity crushes and more than man enough to handle a diva. He doesn't preen or pose, he's matter-of-fact and down-to-earth. And underneath the tough exterior there's a vulnerability. Liam is a man I know I could take home. He'd behave himself and he'd look after me, buy my mum flowers and help my dad with any heavy lifting. I've thought this through, can you tell? I spend time thinking about Liam every day. There's a thing in positive psychology called creative visualisation. The theory goes that if you imagine something often enough and hard enough, eventually it happens because you've willed yourself to make it happen. Well, I'm creatively visualising Liam now and I can almost smell him.

Gerard Butler

Like a Scottish version of Liam, Gerard Butler is still rough around the edges, but a little more refined. Usually I like a chick flick but I'll happily watch Liam or Gerard in an action movie. Gerard gets Mum's vote too and that's a big plus because I don't think I'll ever be allowed to settle down with a bloke unless he gets The JC's blessing. Gerard looks like he's man enough to handle an uber-diva like myself and also chilled enough not to care too much. There has to be a delicate balance with me between a man who will do what I want him to do and a man who will tell me to pack it in when I'm playing up. It is a balancing act. A bloke has to be able to read me and know when I'm being serious and when I'm being playful. It's my prerogative to be fickle; a real man will be able to work me out. Gerard started his career as a lawyer so he's got some smarts about him too and hasn't grown up surrounded by showbiz, so I reckon he's got his feet on the ground too, which is a bonus.

Tamer Hassan

'Who?' I hear you say. 'Oi, you leave my Tamer alone!' OK, so he doesn't have the profile of Liam or Gerard, but if they were not available then I'd settle for Tamer. For those of you who don't know who he is, Tamer is an English actor of Turkish Cypriot descent. He is best known for his role as the leader of the Millwall football hooligan firm in the movie *The Football Factory*, in which he starred with Danny Dyer, who seems like a nice bloke but who is a bit short for me. I've liked Tamer for years and was over the moon when he turned up in *Game of Thrones*, one of the only two box sets I've ever watched. That's what you call fate. I also like the fact that his son is named Taser. Anyone who names their kid after a non-lethal police pacification device gets my vote. I once went out with a bloke who looked a bit like Tamer. But he was a ponce and waste of space so it didn't work out.

Tony Soprano

Ah, Tony. If you asked me a few years ago who my ideal man was, I would have told you he was a cross between Tamer

Hassan and Tony Soprano. Anthony has everything a diva needs in a man: strength, loyalty, some vulnerability, his own profitable waste disposal company, power and a friend called Big Pussy. What's not to like? OK, so he's also the ruthless boss of a New Jersey mafia family, but no one's perfect. I watched most of *The Sopranos* shows and grew more in love with Tony over the years. I think it was because he reminded me of so many of the older blokes in Essex. They're all duckers and divers, most of them have car dealerships on pieces of wasteland and you very rarely see them clean-shaven. Like everyone else who loved Tony Soprano, I mourned when *The Sopranos* ended and shed a tear when he died at the end of the last episode . . . or did he? They never showed him being shot, did they? So perhaps he's still alive.

Paul Hollywood

Those eyes! One sexy stare from Paul Hollywood's peepers could melt a pavlova from 100 metres. I don't know how Mary Berry worked with him for so many years and didn't give in to her primal lust instincts, she must be the ultimate professional. I know for a fact that if I ever got the gig judging cakes with Paul, I'd struggle to keep my hands off his cream horn. I mean really, what more do you want from a man? He's got a lovely soft accent (I think it's from up north somewhere), he's got eyes that look like jacuzzis and when you're done with him, he'll knock you up a batch of fresh donuts.

Robbie Williams

I loved all the Take That boys, but Robbie was my favourite because he was the bad boy of the bunch. Since I've been famous I've not met him even though I would love to. Showbiz is a small world and at some point our paths will probably cross. He's a happily married father now so we've both missed the opportunity, which is sad but that's life. There have been moments where I've crossed paths and bumped into a few of the other Take That lads when we've been in the same TV studios or at the same events, but obviously I've styled it out like a diva and not acted like a big fan, which is properly nerdy. I just breathed deeply and although I knew they were there, I told myself: 'Gem, you are so famous yourself now, they should be feeling nervous in *your* presence.'

Men: a shopping list

A diva needs to set standards when she's choosing the right man. It's best to have these written down somewhere so you can tick them off one by one as you get to know your fella, like a shopping list or a game of bingo. Be realistic, obviously. If one of your requirements is that a man has his own yacht and island hideaway, you may well end up on the shelf, surrounded by cats and loneliness. I have a set of minimum standards and although blokes may say I'm high maintenance, I reckon I'm easy to please. The most important requirements are that a geezer has to make me laugh and has to fill the car up every week with petrol. If he can't make me smile and put £70 of petrol in the tank, he needs to get out of my life. I'm not materialistic and it's certainly not all about money, but I need to know that there is some level of equality. Sadly, when you get to my level of fame, you discover that the male world is full of liggers who are looking for a meal ticket, and that ain't me. Once he's passed the Texaco test, there are other qualities that I look for too:

Power

Divas are hard to handle and it takes a man who is used to power to contain them. Power is like an aphrodisiac, it's why politicians seem to punch above their weight when it comes to the women they attract. Let's be honest, Lembit Opik would never have been able to pull a Cheeky Girl if he was a bus driver rather than a politician (not that there's anything wrong with bus drivers), and would Melania have married Donald Trump if he worked in B&Q? Probably not. Power comes with great responsibility and a powerful man should be a kind man as well.

Chivalry

Whoever says chivalry is dead isn't looking hard enough. A diva rightly expects a man to open doors for her and pull out chairs for her. Standing when she enters and leaves a room might be a bit too much but there's something old-fashioned and nice about it. What woman doesn't like to be made to feel special? And the good thing is, even if you are with a fella who doesn't do these things automatically, men are trainable. There is a system called positive reinforcement that they respond well to. Whenever they do something good, such as open your car door for you, praise them or give them a little treat. You'll be amazed how quickly they pick things up.

Masculinity

There's a worrying trend towards metrosexuality where every bloke is beginning to look the same in their stretch jean leggings, white trainers and muscle shirts. *TOWIE* has to take some of the blame for this, I'm afraid. Today's blokes are preened, pruned and shaved, with plucked brows and hairless chests and arms, and it's not funny any more. Where have all the men gone? I like a manly man, with chest hair, leg hair, stubble. When I snog a bloke, I don't want his skin to feel smoother and softer than mine, and I don't want him to take longer to get ready than me. A man should always have to wait for a woman to make herself perfect before they go out. Upset that golden rule and you risk upsetting the natural balance of the world. Men should be groomed – smart, clean, fresh – but not overly groomed. Male grooming has absolutely gone too far; men should be men. It's OK for a man to take pride in his appearance but as for Botox and fillers and all of that, it's absolute crap.

Respect

This is a biggie in any relationship. You have to care for each other and respect your differences. The best partnerships bring out the best in both individuals. They revolve around respect and support. I base my ideas about what a perfect relationship should be on my parents' marriage. They recently celebrated their ruby anniversary and they still make each other laugh. They understand each other 100 per cent and they encourage and look out for each other. Their relationship is very special. Perhaps that's why I've never found the right bloke. None of the relationships I've had measure up to the benchmark they've set.

Mystery

Closeness and intimacy are lovely, but there must be mystery too. I can't stand it when I hear couples talk about how they are so close they leave the bathroom door open and have a chat when they take a shit. It makes me want to barf. Why would you want to see that or be anywhere near it? What are you, some kind of a pervert? The key to a harmonious relationship is this? You should never share a bathroom. Whoever I marry will have his own bathroom and will not be allowed anywhere near mine. You don't need to know what I'm doing in there. And we would certainly not be sharing the same toilet. My husband will have his and I'll have mine. In an ideal world we'd have separate floors. He would have his own rooms, so would I, and when we wanted to be together we would have a shared space. We would share the kitchen and sleep in the same bed but also have the option of separate beds because there's nothing wrong with wanting your own night's sleep occasionally. Space is key. Everyone needs their own space to breathe and be an individual; you can't be joined at the hip 24/7. I'd draw the line at separate houses, though. My man needs to be around me, as and when I choose to have him.

Emotions

There's something nice about a man who isn't afraid to show his emotions. Vulnerability should be celebrated (in small doses). A man needs to be strong and he needs to be able to look after his diva but when he needs help, he should be confident enough to ask. It's OK for men to cry in public. They should cry more often. It shows they are human. It's nice to see a man cry when you haven't caused it or when some terrible tragedy hasn't happened. A man who can sit in front of his lover watching *DIY SOS* and cry when the family comes back for the big reveal and sees what all the neighbours have done to their semi is a man in touch with his emotions. Happy tears, sad tears, just tears; men shouldn't be scared to be emotional, within reason of course. You don't want your bloke to get all weepy over silly things. And he also needs to realise that he needs to be supportive when you are feeling emotionally fragile.

James 'Arg' Argent

(Sigh.) What am I going to do about James? For readers who live on Mars and don't know who I'm talking about, James is Arg, a *TOWIE* cast member that I have a special link with. We have been a running item for several years. We are the classic on-and-off couple. As I'm writing this, we're off, but also sort of on. It changes by the week. Perhaps, in time, we'll resolve our differences. We've been good friends for years now and there's a strong bond between us without a doubt, but it is complicated.

Everyone seems to be rooting for us to be a couple and that is really sweet. The thing is, we've been through so many ups and downs that we have this really strong shared history, which means we have a lot in common. But then we are also very different. I'm sorry I can't be much clearer than that, but the truth is, it's complicated and I'm not sure I need complication in my life.

I could see there was an attraction between James and me when we first met in 2012. James and me had chemistry. We make each other laugh. It's never been about looks for me, it's about personality, and when James is on form, he's lovely company.

Me and James shared one of TV's most iconic moments when I was in full GC mode by the poolside in Marbella and told him: 'You ain't ever getting this candy.' He'd been disrespecting me by talking to his mates about our private life so I gave him both barrels. No one disses a diva! It was a liberating moment and afterwards, Arg was like a kid, having a paddy because I mugged him off. Secretly I knew he loved it though. There is a seven-year age gap between us and sometimes it shows. He's quite young for his age too, so I can crush him in two minutes with my wit and bants.

We've shared some lovely times, but there has also been a lot of heartache though he's always been a friend. He can be a real sweetie – he bought me kissing fish and we've spent some lovely times together on holiday in Spain, in beautiful hotels and with my family at Christmas.

There is still chemistry and there will always be a part of me that wishes I was twenty-four or Arg was thirty-one, because I probably would have been with him if he was older, more stable and mature. Arg is like a safety net but he isn't the strong man who will protect me. It would probably be the other way around. I need someone who is big, muscly, who stands by my side.

Celebs Go Dating

Thanks to my complicated romantic history, a while ago I was approached to do a series called *Celebs Go Dating*. The show had form with the *TOWIE* cast because previously Joey Essex, Arg, Bobby Norris and Ferne McCann had done it. 'Why not?' I thought. It was a popular series and seemed like a fun thing to be involved with. The idea of the show was to set a selection of single celebrities up on a series of dates with different members of the public. There were a couple of dating experts on hand to give advice and offer analysis after each date.

On *Celebs Go Dating* I was set up with a series of blokes that I was obviously not going to get involved with on a romantic level in any way at all. There was Terry, the one who called me a diva as an insult, then there was a bloke who lived with his mum, couldn't pronounce the word 'prosecco' and whose ultimate fantasy date venue was an eat-as-much-as-you-like Chinese buffet. What was he going to offer me, apart from endless spicy Szechuan chicken wings and indigestion?

On one of the first dates I walked out because it was that obvious that the evening was DOA. Sometimes you can salvage a date. Other times something happens or something is said and it becomes very clear that it will never work romantically. If you are having a laugh and enjoying the company then it's fine to stay. But if you have nothing in common at all – or worse, if there's a tension or you clearly don't like the other person – then don't waste your time. Make your excuses and go, even if the bloke fancies you. If you ain't feeling it, get out of there.

There's never a good way of letting anyone down. You just have to be brave, be bold and swerve it. A diva can't waste her time because she only has limited time on this planet to be fabulous. Never be rude: always do it with a smile, like a smiling assassin. Be honest, be frank and deliver the blow kindly but firmly. If you're not honest in the first place and you persist with a date when you know it's never going anywhere, you'll spend the next weeks avoiding his calls and messages and eventually have to let him down anyway, so it's best to get it over and done with sooner, rather than later. And then ghost him on social media.

Anyway, on *Celebs Go Dating*, after a few false starts, I was eventually matched up with a bloke called Laurence Hearn, who was really lovely. After the show I spent some time with him and he came round to my house and helped me out when I moved. He's a handyman so he also helped out in my shop when I opened a second one. He is a really great guy. I appeared on *Loose Women* after *Celebs Go Dating* finished and Laurence was in the audience. I was honest and mentioned that Arg had been in touch and had asked me out on a date. All the headlines said I'd dumped Laurence live on air.

On Valentine's Day Laurence delivered a lovely bunch of flowers to my door when I was out and then sent me a picture of him delivering them. I'm sure his intentions were noble, but it did make me think. Flowers are supposed to be surprises, especially on Valentine's Day. Why would you tell someone you had delivered them and send them a photo if you didn't want to advertise it and let people know what you were doing? Don't get me wrong, Laurence is a really nice guy, but he's not the one for me.

People ask me whether I learned anything from *Celebs Go Dating* because there were experts on it giving advice. Honestly,

I learned that maybe I should open up a bit more and that if a man thinks the height of haute cuisine is unlimited prawn toast and lemon chicken, it's time to get the bill.

Sex and flirting

What happens in a diva's bedroom stays in a diva's bedroom. A diva and her girlies like a gossip about blokes, but she remains discreet and is far too classy to go blabbing about her love life to anyone other than her closest mates. Divas don't do home sex tapes as a rule, and if they do, they make sure they own the only copy and that it's password-encrypted and stored securely.

One-night stands happen. That's a fact of life and I'm not out to judge anyone. All I'll say is that a one-night stand doesn't really set the right footing for a stable relationship. If you give up the goods too soon, your bloke will lose interest. You are worth waiting for and you've got to make them want that candy and work for it.

Be fun, be flirty, give off the right vibes but be coy too. You want them to know you are interested but not to the point where they don't have to try. Eye contact is sexy, but don't stare, that just freaks people out. There is something called mirroring that people do naturally when they are interested in someone. They mirror the other person's movements. Try that, as it gives off subconscious messages, but don't go over the top. If you are talking to a guy and he picks his nose or scratches his bollocks, do not copy . . . walk away.

Divas don't beg and they don't chase; they let the fella do the running. Some people say it's old-fashioned but divas like to be treated. We are more than equals with our fellas but we do deserve to be worshipped. Men should make the effort when it comes to being with a lady.

I was a late developer when it came to sex. I first did it with a guy called Jamie at a friend's mum's friend's husband's forti-eth birthday party. Jamie was good-looking. I wasn't really ready to do it but most of my mates had. Jamie was older and I bought a sexy little black and white Morgan dress with which to seduce him. Like most girls' first experiences it was awk-ward, weird and exciting all at once. Afterwards, I felt really proud that I had done it. I wouldn't say I enjoyed it in terms of the physical side, but psychologically it was a hurdle that I had jumped on the way to adulthood. We did it upstairs in one of the bedrooms while everyone was downstairs partying. I remember the song 'Return of the Mack' by Mark Morrison was on at the time. I saw Jamie a few times afterwards, but like Mark Morrison, he was ultimately a one-hit wonder.

The One

Will The GC ever find The One? Fuck knows. I've always met the wrong men in the past. I don't know why. I have always been naïve, and I've always given more than I received.

Basically, at the moment I write this, I'm actually quite happy on my own. But that changes from week to week. I get a lot of male attention when I'm out and I can it take it or leave it. I'm not obsessed by men. I never go out with the aim of meeting a fella. I go out for me, for my girls and to have fun, not to find a man.

My mum always says: 'I don't know if you will settle down and have kids.' She isn't judgemental about it and she might be right. Society tends to view single childless women in their thirties and beyond as a negative, but that's wrong. If it's not for you, it's not for you. The most important thing is to be happy and true to yourself, and I'm lucky that I have family and friends who understand that and don't have expectations. I know some girls whose parents are desperate for grandchildren and are forever trying to set them up with prospective husbands. Thankfully The JC has such high expectations for me that she has just as much trouble finding someone I should be with as I do. When it comes to guys, she's my biggest critic. 'Why are you mixing with this one or that one?' she'll ask, after I've had a cheeky weekend with a scaffolder. And I tell her that sometimes I just need a bit of reality. I need to be mixing with someone who works as a scaffolder and is from a council estate in East London. Instead, she wants me with a royal. The only bloke she'd ever try to set me up with would be Liam Neeson. I wouldn't say no.

The more famous I get, the less chance I feel I will have of finding Mr Right. My life is a whirlwind of glamour and excitement and I'm not prepared to compromise that for a man. In the past I've had relationships with men who just can't handle how fabulous my life is. They get jealous of the attention I get and feel threatened by my celebrity. I understand. It can't be easy living with a legend. The bigger I get, the more important it is that a man will have to slot in with me and my life. And that will probably end up being someone completely removed from the showbiz bubble I live in but who is at the same level as me. I'm not out there saying I need a billionaire; I ain't looking for a Bernie Ecclestone – he's too short for me anyway – but long-term I do actually need to be with someone I can be equal with. I'd like to end up with a country landowning bloke, someone who has a nice Barbour jacket and some land and who isn't bothered about my work or fame or any of that. I'd like to settle down with someone who loves Gemma Collins more than he loves The GC, but who can handle both. A strong, loving, caring man who looks after me, who has a bit of class and finesse and who knows how to fix a fence and make a dry-stone wall.

If I use my psychic powers and look into the future, I think I'll settle later in my forties because I don't feel old yet and I don't feel ready. Now is not my time to settle. Let's face it, in my circle there are loads of woman my age either bored to fuck with their lives or divorced and starting out again. That's the way life works now. People get married, have a family, get bored and do it all over again in their thirties and forties. All I've missed is a divorce and a load of aggro.

If I do eventually find The One, however, my ideal wedding would be an evening affair because I'm a night owl so it would start at about 6 p.m. I'd probably have it in Cannes now, rather than Marbella, because I'm going up the fame ladder and Cannes is classier. I'd do it in the Hotel du Cap just up the coast in Antibes. It would be fabulous and classy, not chintzy, with lots of white, lots of flowers and my nearest and dearest. I wouldn't have celebs at my wedding; no fucker could ever outdo me anyway. It would be solely for family and friends. I'd probably do a mag like *OK!* or *Hello!*, or *Vogue*. And then I'd live happily ever after, as long he never cheated. If a man cheats, fuck him off basically – it's his insecurity, not yours.

The basics

Basically, love is complicated, and divas are complicated women, which means a diva's love life is like a tricky mathematical equation. Once you get the right answer, however, everything falls into place. The secret to a successful relationship is to know what you are looking for in the first place, but don't be so focused on one type of bloke that you ignore all the others. And don't be defined by a man. You are your own boss and you must stand on your own two feet. You are equals.

Top tips:

★ It's great to have a fittie, but a diva doesn't need a man, she wants a man.

★ If a relationship is going to work, you both need to be on the same level, mentally, physically and, ideally, financially.

★ Avoid one-night stands.

★ Make sure your man is man enough to handle you.

★ You have the right to be treated right. Train him up if he's a bit rough around the edges.

★ Keep some mystery in the relationship by keeping the bathroom door closed. He doesn't want to see you sitting on the throne any more than you want to see him.

Chapter Eight
BRAND DIVA: SELL YOURSELF

Ever since I can remember, I always wanted to make a pound. I don't know what it is; it's in my blood I guess. I love doing a deal. I always want to make a sale, whether it's 50p, £5 or £500. If I've made something, I'm happy. It's the Essex in me perhaps. We are a region of entrepreneurs, always looking to make a buck, to pocket some Benjamins. I love the art of the deal, whether that's selling a uniquely crafted summer dress in one of my boutiques, signing off on a showbiz contract or haggling with a looky-looky man on the Costa Blanca. I was born to make money. Most of my jobs have been in sales. I worked in a shoe shop, in recruitment sales, in motor sales and now I sell the most valuable commodities of all – I sell myself and I sell the diva dream. Line up, ladies, take a ticket, there's plenty to go round!

I get my business acumen from my dad. He sorts out all my financials and makes sure I pay my taxes and stay on the straight and narrow. We have a brilliant relationship. Businesswise he's the safe one, I'm the wild card. I'm the one who can generate the money and get it going, he manages the back end, studies the books and gets involved in my ROIs, my KPIs and my PAYEs. He's also the one who regularly tells me: 'Don't waste the money.'

I love him to death, but honestly, he can be a bit of a tight-arse sometimes. I know he's only looking out for my interests, but if it was up to him I'd be squirrelling everything away in a pension fund and living like a pauper. Take Christmas, for example. I worked like a dog all year and thought I'd have a little shopping session in Harrods. Nothing fancy (and believe me, you could have a proper splurge there if you put your mind to it) but I spent a fair bit on gifts for the family. I like to spread it around and treat my nearest and dearest. It was the season of goodwill, after all. Dad gets all my accounts, so I can't hide anything from him. He doesn't trust my money management since he had to bail me out of my credit card debts. Anyway, a couple of days after my shopping trip I got an email from him. He'd cut and pasted my bank statement and written: 'This is unnecessary spending, I don't want to see this again.'

I wouldn't mind if I was living beyond my means and

spending thousands a week on fresh flowers and Evian baths, but I probably spend £50 a week on shopping. Some nights I'll have a jacket potato with beans or a bit of egg on toast in front of the telly. I'm not living a lavish lifestyle. Every so often there are days when I'll go: 'Fuck it, I fancy a bit of lobster today', and I'll go for lunch and have a lobster. But when I do I'm always aware that the old man is looking over my accounts and when I get lavish I have this little voice in my head that says: 'Better rein it in a bit, Dad will give you a bollocking.' My dad makes his shoes last three years. He is not tight, he is a very generous man, but he can tell you how much his shoes have cost him and he divides the price of the shoe over the timeframe of wearing them to work out their profit value.

I work hard and play hard. I have never been scared of rolling up my silk sleeves. Even in *TOWIE* we put in the hours. I've always had jobs and never been a scrounger. A diva has self-respect and can stand on her own two feet. Sure, some divas end up marrying rich men and live their lives as kept women, and that's fine if that's what they want. But a diva will never rely on a man and will always have her independence. A diva has the smarts and the work ethic to earn for herself. If she doesn't have to or doesn't want to, that's fine, but the important thing is to always keep your ability to be independent. By all means marry a millionaire and let him look after you, but never rely on anyone apart from yourself.

I thank my dad for my work ethic. When a job needs doing, he has always knuckled down and got on with it. I remember when he was first starting his shipping business and he worked all the hours he could to make a better life for his family. He worked six days a week, sometimes seven when it was busy, and I used to go to work with him on a Saturday when I was little. We'd jump in his Ford (he came from Dagenham where there was a massive Ford plant and Fords were in his blood) – and head to the Isle of Dogs where his warehouse was. I rocked up in my pink fluorescent off-the-shoulder top and my cut-down jean shorts and just messed around all day. I really thought I was a pop star in that outfit and I basically was just really happy to be at work with my dad. He worked so hard; I remember one time he was ill but still managed to get into work. He was literally lying on the floor taking calls, in agony but soldiering on. It turned out he had pneumonia. He could have killed himself. Because he set the business up, he did everything himself and as it expanded he always took the pressure on his shoulders.

I'm the same now. I'll push myself to the limit and will put in the graft. I don't really have weekends off. If I have a day off, it's not really a day off, it's just a day away from filming and I'll go and work in one of the boutiques I own. I work 24/7, round the clock. Ultimately, I am a grafter. I'm not a woman who can just go out and do lunch every day. I'm not a diva who's sitting back on my laurels, ordering up white roses wherever I go. On an average day, I will get up at 6 a.m., film, get back late, lie down for two hours, get back up, shuzz my make-up and go to a club to do a PA. People think when you're on a reality show all you do is just sit on your arse for half the year and then swan around looking glamorous for the other half. In fairness, there are plenty of people in telly shows who do just that. But I realised early on that I had a brand to build and that's exactly what I've done. *TOWIE* was a great opportunity and provided a springboard from which I launched myself into the swimming pool of global success. Most of the others just dip their toes in now and again, and don't know how to swim. Me, I'm in the deep end.

Brand GC, my empire

One of my proudest achievements is my clothing line, The Gemma Collins Collection. I sell beautifully designed garments to a global marketplace and have two boutiques in Brentwood in Essex, where you'll sometimes find me manning the till and helping girls to look amazing. I love going to my shops and I'm a hands-on mogul. I make all the big decisions and plan my own business strategy. I'm juggling a load of balls and spinning plates at the same time. I have my fashion empire to run, my showbiz career to keep pushing forward and I'm still working on other projects. I want to act, I want to do movies and give Hollywood a go, plus I fancy writing and starring in my own musical. And I plan to start doing a range of interiors too. I never really have time to just take stock and enjoy all the things I've built because I just want to keep moving forward.

I keep myself grounded by going to the shop and meeting my customers, plus when I'm there it's good for business. There were rumours that I used to charge people £10 for a picture if they came into the shop and wanted a photo with me. Believe me, if that were true, I'd be a billionaire by now. The truth is we used to get so busy with queues of people wanting pictures while there were also people who wanted to actually buy the dresses, that we used to say anyone buying the products would take priority. Anyone wanting a selfie with me would have to get in another queue and I'd see them when I was done serving the paying customers.

The shops have been a massive success and have lasted longer than several other *TOWIE* businesses, but that's because I built myself into a brand. We clothe women who look at me, admire my confidence and want to be divas like me. The formula has been a huge success, even though my dad never thought it would work. It wasn't the idea of building a fashion brand and owning a boutique that he was against, he just believed I should be out there doing TV. But I knew it would work and that I could do both, so I saved £13,000 to start the business. I said to the family: 'I'm going to open a shop.' The whole family were like: 'That's gonna last five minutes. She ain't gonna concentrate on that.' Well look at me now!

You see, I realised I had to do something when I saw the crazy direction my life was going in. I'm not a muppet and I don't take anything for granted. Fame is fickle, and you can be flavour of the month one week and out the door the next. Luckily, I've established myself so firmly now that I expect I will be famous for the rest of my life, but in those early days I wanted to create a back-up for myself and something that would give my life some normality. When I was little, I always wanted to be a shop girl and work in a boutique so it was natural that when I could afford to I did it and several years later it's still going and expanding. To be honest, I'm not making fortunes but it's early days. There are times when it makes money, times when it doesn't and times when it's fucking hard. But the minute the weather picks up and people come out looking for beautiful pieces to take on their holidays, it's brilliant. In business you have to believe in your brand and your idea and keep plugging away, taking the rough with the smooth.

My ambition now is to take my clothing collection to the rest of the world; I'm talking LA, I'm talking Saint Tropez, I'm talking Bombay, Montego Bay and Montpellier. You name it, I'll be there, making plus size women look fabulous. The reason I see this vision is because there are so many women out there who are plus size and who cannot get clothing to fit them. Being a plus size girl who has been ostracised all her life because I was bigger, especially in TV and showbiz, I realised it was about time someone came along and revolutionised the plus size clothing industry, and that's me. It was my calling. I am the chosen one. From size 18 to 30, I am here to be your saviour and make you look sexy.

There is a real reason behind my passion for fashion. There are shops today that don't allow plus sizes to sit on their floors. River Island just took away their plus size off the shop floor; it's website only. In my opinion that's terrible. It's also very bad for business when you consider that the average size in the UK is 16 and that a quarter of all women are a size 18 or above, and that plus size clothing makes up over 12 per cent of the total UK clothing market. Oh yeah, I do my homework and I know my figures. Deborah Meaden wouldn't be able to tie me up in knots in *Dragons' Den*. Plus size is a growing trend, literally. On top of that, in my favourite New Look store, they put their plus size clothes on the top floor, right at the back. It's like they swept their bigger sizes under the carpet, like they are embarrassed by it. We are being ostracised (which always sounds to me like a fitness class for big birds).

So the fashion brand is a huge passion for me. My main goal is to keep providing amazing plus size fashion for curvy girls.

My website is international, and we get a lot of orders from girls overseas. However, when I have my collection in Bloomingdale's and Macy's in New York I'll know I've really made it. That's the market I'm aiming for. Over here in the UK you can't get plus size designer gear for women. But I was recently in New York and I went into Macy's and there was a whole floor of plus size. A good businesswoman spots a gap in the market and fills it. I've found a massive gap, and I'm a big enough brand to fill it.

How to negotiate

The other day someone asked me for tips on how to negotiate like a diva. I told him straight: 'Honey, a diva doesn't have to negotiate.' Divas get what they want every time. You should never compromise and never let people tell you how to run your business. Take advice from people you trust and from people who know what they are talking about, but the minute someone tries to get one over on you, walk away. Do it nicely, with a smile, because you never know when you're going to run into people again, but never let someone take you for granted. Listen with an open mind but stay true to yourself and your vision. If you stick by your guns, people will respect you and realise they can't get one over on you. All my suppliers in business respect me because they don't treat me as a TV star, they treat me as a business person. I'm sure at first they thought I was a fly-by-night, like my dad did. But I'm still going and still expanding. I've earned that respect.

Business is about knowing your own secret formula, knowing what works and developing that into something that turns a profit. I know how my business ticks and what makes it work, but I wouldn't tell anyone. You find in business when you are successful that you'll get a lot of people coming in and trying to take over. My formula works, that's why I have two successful businesses and an online shop.

Finally, if you ever go into business with a partner, be clear at the outset what you want from the partnership and what you expect, and have a good lawyer draw up a contract.

My business philosophy

Money is not my god, it never has been. Passion for what I do comes before money every time. If I don't enjoy it, there's no point doing it. Mariah Carey doesn't sing because she gets paid millions, she sings because the music is her passion. For her, the money is secondary, although, fuck me, does she know how to spend it.

Even if I won the EuroMillions, I wouldn't spend it all and would give loads of it away first. I'd help a lot of people, give a lot away and make sure my family and friends were OK. I'd help kids with cancer. Cancer and kids are the worst thing that could ever happen. And then, because I'm a diva, I'd have my own yacht and full-on staff every day, like a chef and a maid and a live-in personal assistant. I'd go full-on Oprah style, but make sure people were sorted first.

Like my dad always said: 'Don't be a slave to money.' We all have to work and put in the hours, so you might as well find something you enjoy doing, otherwise you've got a miserable working life ahead of you. There's an old saying that if you do something you love, you'll never do another day's work in your life. It's true – even if you don't do something exciting or glam, find something in your job that you enjoy and concentrate on that.

Divas follow their dreams and thrive on passion, so if you can turn a profit as well, then you are winning. Honestly, my shops probably won't make me a millionaire; they turn a profit and give me a wage, but that's because I don't rinse the business and I keep investing. Some days business is tough, but we always make up for it. It's a long game, and I'll have my shops for years. I don't continue investing in them because I expect them to make me super-rich, I have them because I love them. The brand itself will grow and grow. I already had a collection on Oxford Street in Evans which was a real high point for me given my spiritual connection with the road. It was there for five years but they were taking a large cut, so in the end

I thought: 'Fuck that.' It's what I was talking about earlier: if you suspect someone's taking the rise, walk away.

I'm my own person – I respect other successful business people for their achievements, but I don't admire them, I only admire myself. That might sound big-headed but it's Whitney's rule number one of self-confidence, and divas should live by it. Learn to love yourself.

It's important to be an original, too. A lot of business people look at something successful and copy it. Burger King and McDonald's, Costa and Starbucks, KFC and Chicken Shack. That's fine if you're in it for the money, but a diva strives to be different and to make a difference. She finds her own path. I've got too much enthusiasm and personality to copy anyone else. I always need to be the boss. I'd be good on *The Apprentice*, but I'd need to be sitting where Alan Sugar sits. I'm a free spirit. My own power comes from within. I don't aspire to be anyone or to be like anyone. A diva doesn't aspire to be anyone else other than herself. She doesn't have to charm anyone – they come to her.

My business is me; I am a walking talking business, I am a brand. I am the chairman of the board. I could sit on a toilet seat all day and pull in money. I could walk down Brentwood High Street with 10p in my pocket and turn that into a tenner. I am the money-maker. I drive the business.

I have staff and they love me and respect me. As a boss I am fun. Everyone who works with me has been with me for years. I don't micromanage. People know what needs to be done and if it doesn't get done, I want to know why. Time is key in my life so when I am about, everyone needs to understand what needs to be done and then they need to do it. We all have fun in Brand GC, though. I take my staff out for meals and we have a laugh. People who work for me get the fabulousness and madness that drives me. I couldn't have corporate people working for me; my staff have to be a bit nutty. Everyone is a character and an individual. Everyone who works for me has to have a hint of me in them. At interviews that's what I look for: a little bit of diva sparkle, whether they are girls or boys.

How to dress for business

Dressing for business? The rule is simple. You dress absolutely fabulously. Being a diva businesswoman, I'm not a big lover of black. I celebrate colour. I don't conform because divas are non-conformists. If a diva wants to walk in a boardroom draped in faux fur and Swarovski crystals with a tiara on her head and a big pair of shades, that's fine. She's owning that meeting. Anything goes. She's a diva, that's her right. Just because it's business doesn't mean you have to put on a black suit. You don't have to have a boring business wardrobe. Even if you are not a businesswoman and work in Lidl or KFC or behind the reception at the local leisure centre and you have to wear a uniform, accessorise your name badge with some stick-on crystals and make sure you wear fabulous earrings (if you do work in KFC, make sure the crystals are stuck on properly though to avoid choking hazards). If I have to wear a suit, I make sure it's a power suit in a nice colour with shoulder pads. I only wear black on rare occasions, like at funerals or when Dolly Parton dies (God forbid).

I have the same rule for the people who work for me. If we are selling fashion, we need to look the part. The people in my shops are representing the brand. I'm also not a fan of people in business who get work done on their face and body because they think it gives them an advantage. A diva shouldn't need Botox and fillers. Women should be empowered in their everyday lives without having to feel the need to change their faces and bodies. A diva gets by through force of personality and dress sense; she doesn't have to puff out her lips and stick out her chest to get noticed.

Here are some ideas for how to leave your diva calling card and impress in a job interview:

★ Everyone will be wearing business suits. Go in a gown and top it off with a tiara. Even if you don't get the job, you'll be remembered.

★ Do your research. Make sure you know a bit about the firm. If you know who will be interviewing you, look them up on social media, find out what they like and drop it into conversation, or add it to your CV. 'Ah, Miss Collins, I see you like Roman pottery too . . .'

★ Make sure your bronzer is applied evenly. Too pale and they'll think you are a vegan, too streaky and they'll think you're a zebra.

★ Smile and make eye contact. Even if you're bored, act interested and ask questions.

★ Wash beforehand (I know it's obvious but you'd be surprised).

★ Bring gifts for the interviewer, like a cake. Bribery works.

My CV

A diva needs to try out different things to find out what she wants to do with her life. Divas should never settle for the first thing that comes along. They should be ambitious and always try new ideas. It's all about developing as a person and moving forward.

I've done loads of jobs throughout my life and given every-thing a go. If I hadn't taken opportunities, I wouldn't be where I am today. Before I was famous I had jobs in clothes shops, in offices, in a care home and in the car showroom. I worked in Warehouse and that was fun – I was thirteen and it was my first Saturday job and I really enjoyed it. I worked in the Romford one and later I worked in Benetton, which really pleased my mum. I loved meeting new people, I loved fashion, I loved working the till. That's probably where I developed my love of shop life. And when I worked for BMW I got a thrill from making a sale.

I always wanted to get out there and earn, even though sometimes my mum worried about her little girl going to the big city. When I started working in an office up town, Mum would tell me not to stand too close to the platform on the Underground in case I slipped and fell in front of a train. She put the fear of God in me. Now of course I don't use public transport because I get mobbed when I go out, but for years when I did, the minute I stood on the platform I could hear the dulcet tones of Mum in my head saying: 'Do not stand on that platform, someone might push you.' She also taught me to keep my bag close to me and touch wood I have gone through life without being pushed under a train or mugged, apart from one time when I was a kid in a nightclub when someone punched me and stole my bag. Mum has always told me to be astute, never open my purse in front of people and be on my guard. That's probably why I've never let anyone take advantage of me in my business dealings.

Gender equality

They say that women get treated differently in business and that there is a pay gap. That is totally wrong and should not be happening. Everyone is equal, apart from divas, who are a little bit better than most people. But in terms of gender, everyone should be treated the same and paid the same if they are doing the same job. And anyway, people see me as a bit of an alpha male so they wouldn't try and stitch me up. I don't go out of my way to be like it. I'm naturally ballsy and I say what I think. Some people see that as aggressive but I like to think I am assertive, and there is nothing wrong with that. Sometimes you see businesswomen who try too hard to be blokey. They think they've got to have bigger balls than the men. It looks stupid. Be a woman, that's your superpower. Ultimately a diva knows her worth and she'll only get paid what she knows she's worth.

Looking into my Swarovski crystal ball

Everyone should have a plan, otherwise you drift through life. I've always had a direction and I always know what I want. Some people write their dreams down on a piece of paper and bury it under a tree or burn it and make a wish in the hope that the dreams will come true. I'm not judging, whatever floats your boat, but I prefer to have a plan and work at. I am planning to retire at some point in my forties, so I've got to hit the big time pretty soon. But I'm not going to retire to the point of doing nothing; I'll still maintain my public profile but I'll be selective in what I do. I'm going to step back from TV and build my empire, while also doing a spot of interiors. I'm already researching – me and The JC like to travel around Essex looking at interior stuff. I might devote myself to some charitable work too. I support a local animal charity and maybe I'll go on some fact-finding missions abroad to see how I can train women in the developing world to be divas. I could set up diva academies all over the globe.

The basics

Everyone needs to work (unless you are the wife of a Russian oligarch) so it makes sense to do something you like. If you're already in a job that isn't any fun, either try to find something about it you do like, or change jobs. I know that's not always realistic but if you have to work, you might as well enjoy it. If you work somewhere boring, brighten it up, you're a diva! If you're dealing with the public give 'em a bit of razzle dazzle – even if you're working in the job centre or in a call centre you'll be amazed at the reactions you get when you change the way you are with people. Have a laugh, some banter and a bit of a flirt if it's appropriate and watch how things transform for you.

Top tips:

★ A diva is not afraid of hard work.

★ Follow your dreams and work to make them happen.

★ Do something you love if you can.

★ Know your own secret formula.

★ Dress for success, not for a boring board meeting.

Chapter Nine
DIVA ESPAÑA

*T*he biggest and best divas cannot be confined by geography. They go global. You can pretty much wander anywhere on the planet and show anyone a photo of Madonna and they'll know who she is. Same with Marilyn, Beyoncé and Dolly Parton. They are global icons, a bit like I will be soon. A diva needs to spread her fabulocity around the world. From my base in Essex, I've found the best way to do this is through the internet. Thanks to the online world, anyone can be a global star. Even cats and dogs can be international celebrities now, thanks to Instagram. I'll explain the rules and whatnots of the internet later in this guide but for now, the point I'm trying to make is that the world is getting smaller and a diva needs to travel beyond the boundaries of her own neighbourhood to spread some joy, and also to experience all the glamour that life has to offer.

I know you're saying: 'That's OK for you, Gemma, but I can't afford to jet off on Emirates for a weekend at the Burj Al Arab Jumeirah.' No, you can't. But what you can do is book yourself an Easyjet to Alicante. You owe it to yourself. Everyone has to start their journey somewhere and there are plenty of options for every budget, even if you get a Friends & Family railcard and head to Sandbanks in Dorset. Travelling is one of life's great pleasures and whether for work or holiday, a diva needs to spread her feathery wings and do it the right way.

When I was younger I was never an intrepid traveller because my parents were worried about me too much. When the other kids at school were going off on school trips, I had to stay behind because Mum was terrified some awful tragedy would happen to me. I'm not sure what her problem was as this was in the days before the terror attacks, but she was still petrified for my safety. Her background probably came into it. Maybe she was worried that I'd get lost on a school trip and end up being taken in by a foreign family and be forced to live the rest of my life in Düsseldorf or Rotterdam. I don't think she ever really felt that the teachers were responsible enough to look after me.

The only trip I was ever allowed to go on was to Ypres in Belgium to trudge around graveyards. We got the ferry over to Calais and although the school placed a spending limit of £10 on every child, Dad slipped me an extra £20, just in case I got into trouble and needed some readies. I felt like I'd won the lottery that day. We stopped at a souvenir shop and at the time there was a popular brand called Portofino, which was like Naf Naf, but more continental. The shop was selling Portofino stationery, so I stocked up on a pencil case with matching pens and pencils and felt really grown up. I never thought to haggle at the time and paid the full asking price. I know now that the gear was probably knock-off and that I could have got it for half the price (one of the lessons you learn as you travel more is that legit designer goods are rarely hawked in backstreet kiosks and market stalls).

Another time when I was at school I decided I wanted to go on a skiing trip and my dad paid the £250 deposit. A couple of months before the trip was due to happen me and my parents were sitting in front of the telly at home having dinner when a story came on the news about a girl who had been on a skiing trip with her school and had a terrible accident. I saw Mum's face drain of colour. 'Skiing's very dangerous, Gemma,' she said. 'Are you sure you want to go on that trip? I'm not sure if you'll like it.' The fear started to creep in and eventually I gave my deposit to another girl in my class who wanted to go but who couldn't afford the full asking price. I made some excuse about having a dancing competition I needed to go to instead.

Another time I was at a drama school called Theatre Train

and the owner picked me to represent England in a show in Czechoslovakia. I had to sing Vera Lynn's wartime song, 'We'll Meet Again'. The audience was made up entirely of Czechoslovakians and I don't think they understood what I was singing, but they were all polite and I got a standing ovation. Mum came on the trip with me because she was so worried and wanted to be there to make sure nothing bad happened to me. We stayed in a hostel and it was a dive. The mattress was lumpy, the blankets were threadbare, the pillows smelled damp. I cried because I had never seen anything like it. I was expecting five-star luxury. In the end I kicked up such a fuss I made Mum call Dad and he booked us into a hotel in Prague which was like a palace. The ordeal taught me an important lesson about travelling and being a diva. If you are not satisfied with the service and the accommodation, do something about it, don't just stomach it or you'll be miserable.

Nowadays I make sure I stay in the top hotels and travel business class or better, preferably First Class. I get whisked through airports and barely have to come into contact with normal travellers because I go straight to the lounges where the food and drink are free and where concierges will come and get me and take me to the gate. I realise that sounds big-headed but it is a necessity because I get mobbed wherever I go and if I walked through the normal part of Gatwick or Heathrow, I'd cause a major incident.

The girl's going places

There are a few destinations very close to my heart. Spain always holds fond memories for me because it's where I first started going on my own when I was a teenager. I had a boyfriend called Nick when I was seventeen, and his mum, Pam, was a proper diva too. She used to be a bunny girl in a London casino. She was a character and a half, a stunning woman, dark-skinned and Spanish-looking. She never wore the same outfit twice. The family had a holiday home in Torrevieja in Spain. It was an apartment with a pool. I got on well with Pam who spent a lot of time there and when I finished college she invited me over. I ended up spending loads of time there, going backwards and forwards and I had my first girls' holiday there with Vicky and her little sister Lisa. The highlight of the whole week was going down to Carlos's bar and singing 'Crazy for You' by Madonna on the karaoke. It was one of the best times of my life – a no-frills apartment holiday when I was young and carefree.

My second holiday with the girls was in Ayia Napa. I was into the garage scene at the time which was more glamorous and sexy than the house and trance scene and much classier than drum and bass. We stayed at the Grecian Park, a five-star hotel that was ridiculously expensive. Thanks to our Essex upbringing, me and my mates had been programmed to book the best and I paid for the holiday on a credit card. It was one of the first big spends I made and the start of the eventual debt problems I got into. At the time I didn't care because I was having fun.

Since then I've been all over the world. I'd say that now Tenerife is my spiritual home. I could go anywhere in the world but there is something about Tenerife that I love. I've had some lovely family holidays there and I feel at home there. I go with Mum, Dad, Russell and his family and we sometimes stay at a beautiful place called the Gran Hotel Bahía del Duque Resort. I'm not going to lie, it ain't cheap. I have to stay in places that are exclusive because the more expensive the place is, the more incognito I can be when I'm there. The people who stay in these kinds of places are all loaded or famous, so they aren't bothered about who else is there. Last time we went we stayed in a villa and Michael Schumacher and Keith Lemon were also there. We had two villas next door to each other. You get waited on hand and foot.

I don't take it for granted though and I'm not precious. I've also stayed in the four-star hotel next door and had just as much fun. The thread count on the bed linen and the range of pillows in the pillow menu are important, of course, but it is the people you are with that make the holiday. A diva knows this. She likes her luxury but realises that luxury means nothing if you are lonely.

Hotel heaven

I love hotels, so much so that I could live in them. There's something special about staying in a place where you don't have to do the housework and where you can pick up the phone and order a pizza and prosecco at 2.30 a.m., and someone brings it to your door. I love staying in spas and when I need to recharge, I will often head off to a nice country manor house spa for a couple of days to chill and unwind.

A top hotel is a natural habitat for a diva. Go to the foyer of any five-star hotel in any capital city in Europe and you'll see a constant stream of divas coming in and out with attendants fussing around them. A good hotel knows how to treat a diva. A diva doesn't do incognito when she rocks up at the entrance. Naturally when I pull up at the Dorchester in London, I already know that my car will be taken by the valet and that the bell boy will be ready to take my bags. I don't expect to lift a finger. There are certain standards a diva should expect from a hotel, whether it's the Mandarin Oriental or the Travelodge. These are:

★ Valet parking and car wash
★ 24-hour room service
★ In-room breakfast service
★ Concierge desk

★ Pillow selection

★ Piano in bar area

★ Luxury branded complementary toiletries

★ Quilted loo roll with the corner of the first sheet folded into a point (I have no idea why hotels do this, but it looks posh)

★ Turn-down service in the evening (because a diva doesn't fold down her sheets if someone else is there to do it for her)

★ Electric curtains (see above)

★ Nespresso machine with a selection of pods presented in a velvet-lined dark wooden display case

★ Breakfast choice which includes fresh fruit, at least five types of rustic bread, artisan sausages, choice of eggs (not just a vat of scrambled) and Coco Pops

★ Bone china crockery

I tend to stay in places where they know me so I don't have to faff each time I check in. I'll call up, book and when I get there I'll already be checked in and go straight to my room. When I check out they bring the bill to my room for me so I don't have to go down to reception.

Every hotel I stay in also has to provide a stand-out afternoon tea in a picturesque setting. Divas love their afternoon teas. That's one of my favourite pastimes. There is something about an afternoon tea that just makes you feel special and privileged. That's why I should meet the Queen. We would get on well because we have a lot in common, although I loved Princess Diana and I hear she wasn't so keen.

My favourite British hotel is the Dorchester in London. It is perfectly English and very traditional. There is a good bar and China Tang restaurant downstairs. Every diva should aspire to stay there at least once in her life.

Destination diva

Marbella (Marbs)

Every diva should make the pilgrimage to Marbella at least once in their lives, like Catholics go to Lourdes and Muslims go to Mecca. It's a shrine and place of deep meaning for divas. Perhaps they should do cultural exchanges; they could send the people from Marbella over to Brentwood and vice versa.

Marbella is where Essex goes for the summer. When people say Marbella they actually mean two places in one – there's Marbella itself and a few miles along the coast there's Puerto Banús. Both are full of designer shops, bars, clubs and restaurants catering for wealthy Europeans. Famous clubs include Funky Buddha and Pangea. Marbella has a lovely traditional old town as well if you want some authentic tapas.

The place to be seen is down by the pool where you can have a deal with the looky-looky handbag men. I sat in a bar by the beach once and spent 300 euros on bags, glasses and belts. I had to call security to come down to the pool and carry all the stuff up to the room.

Dubai

Dubai is like a further-away, hotter, more exotic version of Marbs, with added glamour. The hotels in Dubai are something else. Where else in the world can you go up the tallest building on the planet in the morning, lunch like a mermaid in an underwater restaurant, chill by the pool in the afternoon then see Jason Derulo at a nightclub in the evening?

The French Riviera

I've been going to the French Riviera for several years now because I find it a bit classier than Marbella, which has a tendency to fill up with stags and hens every summer. Sometimes you can't walk through Puerto Banús without having to battle through crowds of girls wearing comedy glasses with fake plastic dicks hanging off them and matching T-shirts printed with the bride's face. You just don't see that in St Tropez and Monte Carlo. I ain't being a snob, I love a hen weekend, but when I'm trying to relax with a cold flute of bubbles and some fresh seafood, I like a bit of peace and quiet.

Los Angeles

Hollywood is home to more divas per square foot than anywhere else on the planet. Which is why I plan to move there and break into the Hollywood scene very soon.

New York

I got a taste for the Big Apple when I was flown over to do some promotion work for Netflix. That's what my life is like now. I get calls from big multinationals all the time asking me if I'll do this or that to help them. They want to rub themselves against the GC brand in the hope that some of the glitter will stick to them. NYC was a blast. I turned up and did my job. I was the best I could be and I came away knowing they'd want more. Netflix flew me First Class and put me in the hotel where Jay-Z and Beyoncé's sister, Solange, had a fight in the lift. I had big cars to take me everywhere I wanted to go and I rocked up to Macy's, went up to the seventh floor plus size selection and said: 'Girls, I'm over from the UK and I need some clothes.' It was like a scene from a movie. Americans get me.

Australia

Furthest I've been is Australia, which is about as far as you can go without coming back. I've been twice, once to appear on *I'm a Celebrity Get Me Out of Here Extra*, and then a few years later as a campmate in the actual show. I was the first *TOWIE* girl to get offered *I'm a Celeb* and when I did I knew I was destined to be big in TV because you don't get asked to do the jungle if you aren't a diva like me. The first time I went it was great. I stayed in a lovely hotel and had a good time. The second time I went wasn't so much fun. I'd had some problems, which I'll explain more about later, and I wasn't in the right frame of mind to do it. I've never been one for camping.

Power packing

When travelling, either for work or holiday, you've got to get the look right. Number one is the sunglasses; the bigger the better. These go on before you even get there – you should always wear sunglasses in the airport, except when you are at the passport scanner. Number two is to make sure you take a fabulous range of kaftans in all shapes and colours. Have options with sequins and crystals attached. Number three, gold wedges. They give more stability on a sandy beach. Number four – a big floppy sunhat. Those are the basics.

After that you need to consider a range of night and day wear, including several shoe options, plus beach wear. I can never understand these people who insist on only taking hand luggage and then go away for two weeks with a tiny case on wheels that fits a couple pairs of knickers, some flip flops, a pair of shorts and a vest top. Pay the extra and take hold luggage. When you get to your destination, you need clothing options. I need at least three large suitcases, even if I'm only going away for a few days. I'm not a travel-lite kind of girl. My bags are usually packed for me by my stylist, Lucas, because I'm too busy being fabulous. In fact, I don't think I've ever packed for myself. If I'm going away with the family, Lucas will come around and we'll have a consultation. He'll ask what my plans are at the destination and he will work out loads of outfits for me. I will pick certain items myself if I fancy them, like the mesh swimsuit that I was papped in once when I was away in Tenerife. I picked that out simply because I wanted to wear mesh. Why shouldn't I? If I want to wear a see-through swimsuit, I'll wear it. And the reactions I got were empowering. I like to think that I gave curvy girls everywhere the confidence to be sexy and make their own swimwear choices.

The basics

Travel is one of life's little perks so take the opportunities when they arise. Always remember that you are a diva and, more importantly, you are paying for a service so expect the best and don't settle for anything less. And wherever you go, whether it's Butlins or St Tropez, British Airways or Easyjet, always, always ask for an upgrade and never turn down a complementary drink.

Top tips:

★ Pack for every eventuality. Cabin baggage is for wimps. You have every right to take those twenty kilos of clothes away for your long weekend.

★ Choose your hotel wisely. Do some research. Look on Trip Advisor and check out the customer photographs, not the professional ones.

★ Don't be afraid to ask.

★ Don't be afraid to complain, but be polite when you do.

Chapter Ten

IT'S ALL ABOUT MEME

The internet has changed the world and the way people live their lives. It has made celebrities out of nobodies, it has changed the way we shop, the way we communicate, and it has enabled everyone to talk to everyone else and be an expert in anything. Until YouTube, how many people knew how to peel and cut a mango or an avocado? The first thing you do when you don't know something is Google it.

We are all connected. For most people the first thing we do when we get up is look at our phone. We check to see what the weather is like before we even pull open the curtains and we connect to social media before we do anything else. I happen to believe that the internet isn't all good. First thing I want to do when I wake up is gather my thoughts, not see what

President Trump has tweeted. I don't have any technology in my bedroom apart from a TV. There are no phones or computers or tablets by me when I'm sleeping, it's a no-go techno zone. Anyone who shares the bedroom with me is not allowed to use their phone either. I'm very serious about it. When I'm in my true full-on creative zone I will wake up at three or four in the morning and work through the small hours and I don't want to get distracted by technology. I work through the night because it's quiet and you get a lot done in the still of the night, but social media disrupts that.

I usually have one day in the week when I don't communicate with anyone. That's not me being unsociable, it's just me needing to recharge because being a diva is exhausting. I also don't like the idea that all our devices are now listening to us 24/7. Siri is there in the iPhone, waiting for a command, as is Alexa. I find it creepy. Who knows what they're recording and who's listening in? I think celebs have a more finely tuned sense of security than most people because we've all seen what happens when phones get hacked and pictures get stolen. That's why I won't do phone sex or send naked selfies.

One of the good things about the internet, however, is that it has enabled the world to connect with The GC and share in the fabulousness of my life. TV is great, but the internet extends my reach globally. If the wife of a yak farmer in Mongolia wants to learn about being a diva, she can now Google the word 'diva' and I'll pop up on the screen of her smartphone. The internet enables me to spread the diva message far and wide and to be a force for good in the world.

How to be a mee-may queen

Basically, I never knew what a meme was until one of my girl-friends called and said: 'Gemma, you're trending on Twitter, you're a meme.'

'A what?' I asked.

'Meme. M.E.M.E.'

'I always thought it was pronounced "mee-may",' I said.

I can't even remember what the first GC meme was but for some reason people loved it and ever since I've become the meme queen of the internet. For those like I was who don't know what memes are, they are photos or short video clips with funny captions that are shared on the internet, usually on Twitter and Facebook. The best ones go viral as more people share them and retweet. People make them and send them out in the hope that others will like them.

The whole meme thing started naturally because I think people relate to me and because I tend to react quite dramatically to situations. Most of The GC memes are based on reactions I have to certain things that have been filmed or photographed. For example, there's a tweet with the words: ' "Can

I have a McFlurry please?" Cashier: "Sorry, the machine is broke." ' Attached to it is a two-second video clip from *Celebs Go Dating* of me saying: 'This is awful.' It doesn't translate very well in the written word but Google it, you'll get the idea. Anyway, that meme was viewed almost 30,000 times. Other memes are viewed by millions.

A brief history of the meme (courtesy of the internet)

The name 'meme' was first made up by a bloke called Richard Dawkins in a book he wrote called *The Selfish Gene*. I'm not sure what the book was about – probably romantic fiction about a bloke called Gene who was a bit of a player. When the internet happened 'meme' was used to describe bits of content that spread through the internet from person to person. Usually they are video clips or photoshopped pictures with captions on them, but a meme can also be a catchphrase or an activity, like the ice bucket challenge. There is usually a funny element to a meme, or a shock element. The best ones make people laugh and have animals or little kids in them. They are often quite surreal.

The best way to describe a meme is to imagine a school disco – that's the internet. The hottest boy from the sixth form comes in. He had a cold sore – that's the meme. Give it a week or so, and everyone in school has a cold sore too. It's gone viral because it's been passed from person to person. In a nutshell, that's how memes work. Social media has allowed memes to spread faster than ever and the most famous memes are shared by millions of people. The best way to test if something is a meme is to show it to your gran. If she says: 'I don't get it,' it's a meme.

Famous memes

LOLcats

These were one of the first meme crazes of the social media age. People put funny captions on photos of cats in funny poses. The captions were misspelled, which made the cats look a bit thick. Cats had the last laugh though because the memes are credited with making them the most viewed animals on social media.

Rickrolling

The prank that became an internet craze. Basically, Rickrolling involves embedding a video of eighties pop star Rick Astley singing 'Never Gonna Give You Up' somewhere you would not expect. Props to the Barack Obama White House social media department for great use of the Rickroll in 2011 when someone tweeted that their Twitter feed was boring. To liven it up, the White House tweeted a Rickroll.

Gangnam Style

The Korean pop song 'Gangnam Style' became a meme thanks to its dance routine, which no self-respecting diva would be caught doing by the way. The video of the song (which in 2012 became the most watched video on YouTube) encouraged thousands of piss-takes and copycats, some of which were better than others. Before you could say 'Kim Jong-un', every office, organisation and police force in the world were doing their own 'Gangnam Style' videos and posting them online. My personal favourite was the entire inmate population of a Philippine prison.

Star Wars Kid

In 2002, Canadian teenager Ghyslain Raza made a short video-tape of himself mucking around in a studio at his school, waving a golf ball retriever around as if it were a martial arts weapon. He forgot about the tape and months later some of classmates found it and posted it online to a filesharing network as these were the days before social media. Other people added special effects and sound effects to the video to make it look like Ghyslain was waving a *Star Wars* light sabre around. *Star Wars* Kid was born and the original video is thought to have been viewed over a billion times. The story gets quite sad though because not everyone wants to be a meme queen. Inevitably, online fame comes with downsides and Ghyslain was trolled relentlessly. His parents tried to sue the families of his schoolmates for emotional sufferings and psychological damages. *Star Wars* Kid eventually dropped out of school and ended up in a psychiatric hospital. Today he's a law school graduate and speaks out against online bullying.

Dancing baby

A freaky hypnotic video of animated 3D babies dancing was all the rage in the early days of the internet in the late nineties. The meme started in late 1995 and was originally intended to demonstrate 3D drawing software in the animation world but instead spread as a meme once it was featured on the TV show *Ally McBeal*.

Two girls one cup

2G1C was the first reaction meme. 2G1C was a one-minute video clip of two girls doing something so disgusting and stomach churning that I can't mention it. All I'll say is that if you watch it, you'll never eat chocolate soft whip ice cream again. Honestly, a bit of sick comes up just thinking about it. But that wasn't the point. 2G1C memes didn't show the clip, they showed the reactions of people watching the clip, who were often so confused and horrified, they were hilarious. One person subjected his nan to the 2G1C clip and videoed her reaction. It got over 10 million views when he posted online.

Express for success

There are several Twitter accounts devoted entirely to me and they are followed by people like Alan Carr and Katie Price. The main GC meme account has over 77,000 followers and I love it. The guy who runs it lives in Scotland. His name is Lewis and he's lovely. We've met, and I've brought him down to Essex and put him up in the Crowne Plaza. I saw all the memes he was making and loved them so I got in touch with him. He was surprised and didn't expect anything to come of it as it was his hobby and he was just doing it for something to do. I followed his account and thought they were hilarious, so I Facetimed him and that was it. He even sticks up for me when trolls say nasty things. Basically, if it weren't for him, I wouldn't be queen of the memes. He was the one who has been doing it constantly and now loads of other people have followed. Me and cats are probably the most memed things on the internet. I'm flattered by it because it means people are interested enough to look at me and like me.

The secret to a good GC meme is the reaction and my memes took off after I did *I'm a Celebrity* and then *Celebrity Big Brother*. I was put through so many extreme situations in both shows, I reacted to them in various dramatic ways, which means now if you want a video of me shouting, crying, laughing, screaming, sobbing and every other emotion, it's all there online. There has to be a strong visual element to a viral meme and thankfully I'm blessed with a very expressive face. If you don't put the right reaction to the right caption to make it funny, it won't work. I think I work as a meme because I'm relatable. Lewis says it works because everybody loves me and because there is plenty of drama in my life, which means my reactions are more extreme, which in turn makes the memes funnier. My life is like a meme factory. I even did a video tweet of myself thanking my fans for the memes, and that got turned into a meme.

The most important two rules to follow in order to become a meme queen are:

1. Be dramatic.
2. Don't take yourself seriously.

These are Lewis' tips on how to make a GC meme:

★ Choose a photo or video that shows a big reaction or a very subtle one. Shouting, screaming and any loud noise works well, as does a subtle raise of the eyebrow.

★ The funnier the facial expression, the better.

★ Match the expression to a funny caption. It works best when the original expression/reaction is taken out of context.

★ Put them together in a tweet and send it out into the internet.

Social media sparkle

Social media means I can hook in to my fans direct. They message me and say: 'Hi Gem, what you up to?' and I try to interact with as many as I can, but obviously I get thousands of messages like that every day and can't reply to them all. I wish I could, but I'd be on the phone 24/7 if I did. There's just not enough of The GC to go around. But I find it touching when they message me and say they find me an inspiration, or I've helped them with certain issues in their lives, like they've felt really low in confidence and seeing me conquer and crack on has given them strength to do something with their lives. That means a lot to me because it can be easy to get caught up in the glamour of fame and forget the important things. If I can make a difference to people's lives occasionally, I know I'm doing OK.

My main social media are Twitter – because it's short, easy to use, and it gets me and my messages out to millions – and Instagram, because it's picture-based and equally easy. Social media is a way of letting people into my life. I like to do Instagram Live when I can. I'll walk up the high street and, on a whim, will do a live video. It's a way of connecting with people and opening the glamour window to show them that underneath it all I'm just a normal girl. People watch them in their millions. I have a combined following of nearly five million, which is pretty impressive when you consider that Jesus only had twelve to start with (although he wasn't on Insta or Twitter).

I don't use things like Snapchat and rarely Facebook because I don't have the time to keep up with every new platform. I don't like constantly flogging merchandise on Instagram like some people do, because I think that can look cheap if you do it too much. It's also exploiting fans, which I don't think is right. If I've got some amazing new design in at the boutique, I'll stick it out there but I'll tweet about loads of other stuff too. It's just a way of showing people what I'm up too. I won't lie, I get approached all the time by firms that want me to promote their stuff through my social media feeds but if they want me to endorse something, they have to pay me decent money and I have to believe in the product. Like I've said before, a diva knows her value.

Too much social is a bad thing. I think everyone should take a month off every year and see what it was like when I was growing up and we didn't have any of it. People rely on it too much. Fair enough, some people need it to stay in contact with family and friends and like I said, for me it's a way I can connect to my fans, but it doesn't rule me because nothing could ever rule me. I do worry that we live in a world where we are constantly glued to our phones. If I am with my friends, we have a rule that the first one to pick up their phone and start looking at it or using it pays the bill for the meal. When I am in the room with someone and in a situation, I am there, not somewhere else, so if I'm having lunch with my best friend, everything else can wait. If a friend comes over for dinner and we are having a girly night, the phone can wait. We are missing out on so many things being glued to phones. You can't keep up with all the information and updates that your phone fires at you, so there's no point trying.

Taking the perfect selfie

You are fabulous so naturally you want the world to see how fabulous you are, and that's why God invented Instagram. Why keep all those selfies locked away in your phone when you can release them onto the internet like a flock of exotic colourful birds? Selfies are a way you can express yourself and show the world just how amazing your life is, and if it isn't amazing but is mediocre or even a bit shit, you can lie and pretend that you have a great life anyway. This is why social media is so popular. It gives you the ability to control the way the world sees you. Now you have taken the decision to become a diva, you have a responsibility to make sure that you only take on fleek selfies. Here are some tips:

★ Work out the angles that are best for your face shape. They may be from above or to the side. Photos taken from under your chin rarely look flattering. In some cases, if you are lacking in the looks department, the best angle for you may be from the back.

★ Wear shades if you're tired or your eye make-up isn't working for you. Plus, they make everyone look glamorous.

★ Check your background. Most people concentrate so hard on their selfies, they neglect what's in the background. No matter how great you look in your photo, you'll never be classy if there's a half-eaten takeaway and a box of female sanitary products on the shelf behind you.

- ★ Find a filter that works for you and unless you have a professional lighting rig, natural light is the best way to make sure you have a natural glow when you snap a selfie.
- ★ Practise your pose. It's fine to suck in your cheeks and pout, but it's all about balance. No one wants to look like *Finding Nemo*'s Dory whistling a tune.

Don't feed the trolls

Basically, I ain't gonna waste time on trolls. All I'll say is that there are people online and on social media who like to dish out abuse and try hard to bully people. There's a really easy way of dealing with them. Don't give them any time or energy, never feed the trolls and they starve. I don't pay them the slightest bit of attention and wouldn't even know how many there are trolling me or what they say. On occasion I've even had death threats and it just don't bother me. Trolls don't exist in my world. They are all negative and I do not have time for negativity. If anyone is troubled by them, my advice would be cut them off, cut the cord, ignore them totally. They thrive on attention and are nothing if you ignore them. Simple as.

Sexting and online safety

As your diva guide and mentor, it is my responsibility to make sure you tread carefully through the world wide web. Now, we're all adults here and sometimes, I've heard that it can be fun and exciting to send saucy texts and pics. Not something I'm into, not because I'm a prude, but in my position as a global icon, I have to be discreet and careful. You know what I mean, don't you – Kim Kardashian, Paris Hilton, Pamela Anderson, Kym Marsh, Jennifer Lawrence – the internet is full of celeb sex vids and pictures. I'm not judging, and if it makes you happy then fill your boots, but be very careful who you share intimate details and content with. You might think you can trust him today, but who knows what will happen in the future? This evening's cheap thrill can end up as next week's revenge porn. And once it's on the internet, it's there forever. Ask yourself if it's worth it before you indulge in phone sex. The real thing is usually much better anyway.

Online dating

Swipe left, swipe right, swipe front to back. What's all that about? I've never done Tinder or Plenty of Fish. If that's your thing I hope it works out for you but honestly, I know loads of girls who use those sites and have met lots of chancers and weirdos. A diva needs to be a bit more discerning. If you go internet dating, my advice would be to be honest in your profile, take an amazing photo and consider signing up to a more reputable agency. Even then you can never be sure.

I did try internet dating once. I took to Match.com. I was so embarrassed about having to go on there but I said to my friends: 'I am moving with the times.' I'm old-skool and didn't grow up with the internet and back then online dating had a bit of a stigma attached to it. Now it's where most people hook up, but in my day we went out and met people in pubs and bars. I signed up years ago before I was in *TOWIE* because I was a busy sales executive and didn't have lots of time to go out at the weekend.

My first experience was very daunting but I was having real difficulty meeting anyone and I thought Match.com was my only hope. It was £30 a month. My first date was with a guy called Dan, and he asked me to meet him at a country club and hotel in Hertfordshire. I was nervous about the whole thing and worried that he might have been a serial killer or a kidnapper, so I took a friend. When we arrived and met the guy, I explained that my friend had come along too. He either thought he was in with a chance of a threesome or thought I was a nutter. The three of us had dinner. He was really short and a bit flash. He didn't look like his profile pic at all and he told me he had a private helicopter. It was all bullshit. I didn't believe him one bit. I just thought: 'What the fuck are you doing, Gemma?' In the end I told him I had to leave because I had a really early start in the morning and then waited until he'd gone before booking a room with my friend and having a boozy night laughing about what had happened.

The last word about internet dating is something divas will often come across – dick pics. Sadly, any gorgeous diva who ventures online for romance will undoubtedly experience unwanted dick pics. Block it straight away and do not reply. What is it with men? Do they really think sending a girl a photo of their knob is a good ice-breaker? Most of them have watched too much porn and think that an out-of-focus snap of their sad willy will lead to instant phone sex. I've been sent thousands of them on my direct Insta and I find them repulsive. I am not interested. It turns me off instantly. Please stop sending them, or I'll start naming and shaming. It's inappropriate. I'm an old-fashioned girl at heart, and call me a prude but I can't see how sending a stranger a photo of your knob is romantic, even if you tie a rose to it.

The basics

The modern-day diva can use the internet to spread her fabulousness across the globe. But while social media is brilliant for checking in with your fans and your pals, a diva should use it wisely. Don't over-share and be a social media bore. Instead harness the power of the meme and perfect your selfie poses.

Top tips:

★ Don't be a slave to your phone or social media.
★ Perfect the art of natural-looking selfies and let the diva within shine through.
★ Ignore trolls.
★ Sext at your peril.

Chapter Eleven

BOUNCING BACK: SPRINKLING FABULOUSNESS OVER THE BAD BITS

Life throws all kinds of crap your way no matter who you are. Even divas go through hard times. Heartbreak and bad hair days are a fact of life. They will happen. You can't avoid them. Being a diva means sticking your head above the parapet and telling the world to take notice of you. Inevitably, when you do that, you will face snide comments and jealousy. As Taylor Swift says: 'Players gonna play and haters gonna hate.' Those are the inevitable truths every diva has to face. The trick is to keep standing tall. Don't let the bastards get you down.

I get stick from people all the time. It comes with the territory. I suppose in the old days, before social media, the only way people could get in touch with celebrities was to write to their agents or actually stalk them. Come to think of it, social media has made stalking much easier. Old-skool stalkers had to make an effort. They had to find out addresses, spend time hanging around outside their target's house or the TV studios, they had to invest in things like wrist ties and gaffer tape. Nowadays stalkers can do it virtually from the comfort of their own homes (probably a small bedsit covered in posters of the person they are stalking). I wouldn't even be surprised if there were YouTube tutorials on it. It's lazy stalking. It also makes things very easy for the person being stalked because they can just ignore the stalker or block him, not like in the old days when it was harder to ignore someone who was actually standing in front of you in a mask, carrying a large sack and a syringe full of fentanyl.

Anyway, back to the point of this section. If you can face your troubles, learn from them, keep your sense of humour and your sense of style, and remain gorgeous inside and out during the hard times, then you are a true diva.

This is why it's so important to have a tight group of friends and family around you because when the bad times happen, the people who love you will be there for you. Don't waste your time with people who make you unhappy, spend your time with the ones you can rely on and the ones who make you laugh. As an example, every now and then negative stories get written about me and while there is a bit of truth in the saying that all press is good press, I'd be lying if I said that the negative stories don't hurt. Of course they do; anyone who tells you otherwise is a bullshitter. There is also the added factor that some people seem to enjoy seeing me when I'm vulnerable for some reason. When I get upset by stuff, I turn to my mum for a shoulder to cry on and my mates to cheer me up. I'm not selfish; I'm there for them in their times of trouble too. That's what proper friends do.

Basically, it is OK not to be OK sometimes. I never try and hide it when I get emotional and I am a very emotional person, which is why there are so many memes of me with all my feelings out on display. It is OK to cry in public but always keep your head high and believe in yourself. If you can, turn a negative into a positive. Admit your mistakes but understand that they are not really mistakes, they are just opportunities.

You don't have to be a diva all the time

As I've said before, being a diva is hard work and takes a lot of effort, even if it comes naturally to you. There's no doubt that being a diva is exciting and fun, but sometimes when you've mastered the ways of the diva, it's OK to turn them off and put your diva back in her box. In fact, it is vital that you do. If you swan around in full diva mode all the time, people could well get fed up with you. There is an art to knowing when to deploy your full-on diva powers. Sometimes, no matter how hard you try, you won't be able to be a diva. You may have problems in your life that being a diva will not solve; you may be tired, emotional, sad. It's OK to be vulnerable. You should never hide behind your diva in an effort to avoid something difficult. Sometimes it's more important to be yourself, and then, when whatever the problem you were facing has been overcome, you can flick the diva switch once more and let your inner diva help you heal.

I'm a Celebrity and I got out of there

A good example of turning something which was bad at the time into something which became good was my stint on *I'm a Celebrity Get Me Out of Here!* I was made up when I was asked to go in the jungle. It is a legendary show and I was flattered. I didn't stop to think about the challenges, whether I'd be able to do them, the hunger or the toilet facilities (no folded toilet roll points here). I just said yes because I'm a big believer in taking opportunities when they arise. Say yes first, worry about the details later. Or don't. Fair enough, I like my luxuries, but I reckoned I could rough it. It was only three weeks so what was the worst that could happen?

When you get asked to do the show you go through a bit of a process to make sure you are up for the challenge because it is hardcore. They do starve you and some of the physical challenges can be properly scary. I went in for a meeting with the people who make the show and got accepted. They'd seen me on *TOWIE* and realised I would be TV gold. As the time approached I was looking forward to it but was apprehensive because my mum was ill and I was worried about leaving her. She told me to go and to make the most of the opportunity. She was excited about watching me.

On the plane over to Australia my head wasn't right because I was worried about my mum. I didn't know what to do. I put on a brave face and met up with the rest of the campmates on the first day. I'd heard of some of them but didn't know who most of them were. They seemed like a nice bunch of people. But it didn't take long before the cracks started to appear.

The first problem came when we were taken to a helicopter which was supposed to take us to the camp. I'd never been in one before and no one warned me that I was going to go in one. I got in but I was shaking and I freaked out before it got off the ground. I had a full-blown panic attack, couldn't go through with it and had to be helped out. How the hell does anyone think that's a normal way to travel anyway? They don't even have wings. Of course, everyone watching loved it because it looked like I had cracked at the first hurdle. In truth, I was just a mess and so worried about my mum.

When I got to the camp things didn't get much better because I was sent to the Celebrity Slammer with four other contestants –*'Allo 'Allo* actress Vicki Michelle, Superbike champion Carl Fogarty, Irish model and singer Nadia Forde, and *Coronation Street*'s Craig Charles. We were made to survive on basic rations of rice and beans. People who murder get treated better than that. And that's the truth. Even a murderer gets fed three times a day and has a bit of meat or a treat occasionally. We were just given tasteless food. I have never felt hunger like it. I tried to put on a brave face and I did click with my campmates, especially Craig who I loved because he was a straight-talking, no-nonsense bloke, but it was tough going.

Eventually we got put in with the rest of the camp but by then I was really struggling. One of the big challenges of being on that show is the boredom. Unless you do a trial, there is nothing to do. There are jobs around the camp but for most of the time you sit around doing nothing. Given what had happened, it was the worst place I could have been because all I was doing was thinking about mum. I tried to get involved and I tried to put on my GC mask but I felt myself slipping further and further into a dark place and after three days I had to get out. The biggest challenge I overcame during my time in the jungle was having a proper shit. I apologised for letting people down and explained that I wasn't happy. It was the right decision for me at the time. No one else knew what had happened and so the headlines were all about me quitting. I had to take all the abuse and the stick that went with it for so long after and laugh about it.

Since I came out of the jungle there have been rumours that I'm going back in. The reality is that when I left in 2014 they signed me within three months to go back in the following year because they realised my star draw. I decided that I was going to make a shot of it and try again, but as it came closer to the time I just couldn't bear the thought of ever stepping foot in those jungle toilets again. When I went to see the counsellor that has to analyse campmates and make sure they are mentally well enough to go through with it, she didn't think I should. It wasn't because I was nutty or anything, but she just said she thought it was too much for me. They put Ferne McCann in instead.

It was a really shit situation and it could have affected me mentally and in my career. But I've put it all behind me and anyway, it made people like me even more because the whole thing showed up my frailties and vulnerabilities and my reactions were entertaining. People admire people who go through adversity and come out the other side with the ability to see the funny side. I might not have done a Bushtucker Trial or eaten a kangaroo's arsehole, but I did conquer my demons, and I'm proud of that.

Celebrity Big Brother

Spending several weeks in a house with a gang of celebrities sounds like a laugh, doesn't it? Or maybe not, depending on who you are shacked up with. I mean, if your housemates are Robbie Williams, Mariah Carey, Meghan Markle, Chris Tucker and a token Dreamboy for eye candy, you are pretty much guaranteed the days will fly by. But get the wrong crowd and suddenly your stint becomes more like a prison sentence.

When I was approached to go in the *Celebrity Big Brother* house in 2016 I did my usual thing and said yes straight away, without thinking, hoping that there would be a house full of lovely people to spend a relaxing few weeks with. With diva optimism I thought it would fun. I got a great reaction from the crowd when I went in and felt really positive. I planned to switch on the full GC for the maximum time I was there. The trouble is, The GC is an exhausting character to carry around all the time and as the days wore on, she ground me down.

My housemates were a mixed bag. There were sixteen of us in all, which made it pretty hectic and cramped. I knew a few of them but others I'd never heard of. Like any big group, I liked some more than others. Being cooped up all the time was really hard. It was like doing bird. One thing I learned is that I am very much a free spirit and very much in charge of my own life and I need freedom to express myself and be who I am every day. It's no good for a diva being cooped up all the time. I didn't react well to being told what to do and didn't particularly enjoy getting involved in the games and the tasks. I put my foot down several times and refused to play along, which some people took as arrogance or laziness. It wasn't. I just stood up for myself. I was honest from the outset. I knew it was a game; it's entertainment and I aimed to entertain. It was also boring for most of the time so I caused some mischief with people in there to entertain myself. Some of them got it, some of them didn't.

I lasted for four weeks and was the seventh one to be voted out with just three days to go. When I came out there were some mixed reactions from the crowd but, like I've always said, The GC is a Marmite character. Some people love her and realise that she's not to be taken too seriously, others hate her because they think she genuinely believes some of the things she does. The GC is outrageous sometimes, but when she is, it's always with her tongue planted firmly in her cheek.

When I did my exit interview with Emma Willis, I was honest and explained that I'd had an amazing time but that there were others in the house who deserved to stay in longer because they were better at the tasks. I took the boos as a compliment because there's always got to be a pantomime villain. I explained that for much of the time I was being The GC. Emma wondered whether I would have won if I had been less GC and more Gemma. Maybe, maybe not. But Gemma is a private person, whereas The GC loves the crowd and the reaction. I think the viewers got much more out of The GC than they would have out of Gemma. Whatever the reaction, I walked out with my head held high and kept smiling because that is what a diva does.

There were loads of positives for me and I look back on the experience with fondness. I'm so glad I got to spend a bit of time with David Gest in the house. We had a fond friendship and he really got me. He'd been married to Liza Minelli so he understood the diva mindset. We had some lovely chats and I missed him when he left after two weeks on medical grounds. When I heard he had died a few months later I was devastated.

I also got on really well with Darren Day, who is a lovely guy, and Danniella Westbrook was great fun too. We chatted a lot and actually got on well. The edits showed the flashpoints because the programme needs drama, but the reality is that you are all in there together twenty-four hours, seven days a week and of course there will be rows, but they get resolved and generally everyone got on.

The real highlight for me was meeting Jonathan Cheban. Who'd have thought The GC would ever hook up with Kim Kardashian's best mate? That's why it's so important to say yes, and to grasp opportunities when they arise. They may be hard at the time and you may wonder what you're doing but I believe in fate and, if you are positive, life usually works out for the best. When Jonathan went, I hit a real low in the house because he was my rock. We met up after I came out and have gone on to have a great friendship since being on *Big Brother*. Whenever he comes over to the UK we meet up for a meal and a gossip. He's a real star and I'm hoping that at some point me, Jonathan, Kim and Kanye will meet up. I think they'd love Brentwood.

Making a splash

I try and keep fit, but if I'm honest I ain't the most athletic person in the world. I'll go to the gym and do some training, but mostly I don't. It's hard to find the time. So when I was asked to take part in a reality diving show called *Splash!* in 2014, I knew it would be a challenge but I was up for learning a new skill. I mean, I've jumped off a springboard on holiday before so I'm familiar with the concept of jumping into a pool, but I just didn't have the technique. Tom Daley was the trainer so I couldn't have asked for better expert advice. I was more worried about choosing the right swimwear for the occasion.

The show was a competition format where a group of celebrities make a series of dives which are judged by a panel and by the public. The contestants are gradually eliminated until one wins. When the contestants I was up against were announced, I realised that I wasn't going to win. The group included three professional sportsmen and the amazing little acrobat from Diversity, Perri. But in true diva style, I put a smile on my face and resolved to style it out.

I won't lie, it was fucking awful. The practice almost killed me and I broke down several times. Even the sight of Tom in tiny budgie smugglers wasn't enough to cheer me up. The worst thing about it was the injuries. I flopped a couple of times and bruised my tits. By the time I went on the live show my chest looked like it had done ten rounds with Mike Tyson. I held my head high, wore a gorgeous sequinned swimsuit with a sheer wrap-around to cover my injuries, and put in a good effort. I was terrified and said a little prayer before I launched myself. I did OK considering I was carrying an injury and my dive was described as graceful. I didn't get enough points to go through to the next round though and I was the third person to be eliminated. I've never been so pleased to leave a show in my life! My boobs healed, and I left with my head held high. The whole experience was positive though because, having seen what I went through, I got a great reaction from the public.

The fall of shame

When I got asked to present an award at BBC Radio 1's Teen Awards I almost wet myself with excitement. As you'll discover in a bit, that initial level of enthusiasm proved to be an omen.

The awards took place at Wembley Arena in 2017 in front of a massive live audience. I knew it was going to be one of the biggest moments of my life. They don't just ask anyone; they get the *Who's Who* of icons out when they make the guest list for it.

I planned everything out in detail because I wanted to be the best I could be. I planned my hair, my make-up and my out-fit. Normally I'm not so organised, but this was a big deal and needed some GC strategic organisation. I booked a hair and make-up artist and went to bed early the night before to make sure I was fresh as a daisy the following day.

I got up bright and early, full of excitement and anticipa-tion. Things started to go Pete Tong after my Weetabix when I was presented with the disastrous news that the hair and make-up artist had cancelled. I was like: 'Shit, what am I going to do?' But then I told myself to pull it together. 'You can do your own styling, Gem,' I said to myself. As it was a teen event I wanted to look current so I put my hair into two little space buns to try and look like a teenager and chose a dark floral print top, faux leather leggings and a dinky pair of black trainers with chrome trim. I looked the bollocks. I left with plenty of time to spare and drove myself there in my Mercedes. All the way there I was like: 'OMG, this is amazing.'

When I reached the venue someone pulled me aside and explained that they wanted me to do a live link with Rita Ora. She would walk down a corridor and I had to burst out of the room I was in and start dancing in front of her. It was all go-go-go, quite rushed and panicky. I met Rita, who was amazing and said she was a big fan of mine, and we did the link. Then I was told to go on stage and present the award. It was all so crazy and mad and fast. The truth is that before I went on, one of the girls backstage who was organising things told me to stand on my marker (which is a bit of tape on the stage that tells you where you should be). She didn't tell me that if I moved off my marker I would fall down a hole. She explained that I would read out the name of the winners of the award and implied they would then come on the stage from behind me.

When the time came for me to do my bit I was buzzing. The arena was full and the noise from the crowd was deafening. I stepped out from backstage and basked in the glory and adulation. There was a walkway leading through the crowd to a small circular stage. I walked to it as the crowd screamed. It was like a homecoming. All those years of drama school and singing and dancing slotted into place. I was where I belonged. I fucking loved it and I played to the crowd.

The award I was presenting was for best TV show. I did my introductions, riled the crowd up a bit more and I announced the award. I opened the envelope. I shouted out the name of the winner. *Love Island*! The crowd went mad. I spun around to greet the winners, who I assumed would be walking on behind me.

What happened next became one of the most viewed and shared videos of the year. The cast of *Love Island* didn't walk out from backstage. They emerged from under the stage in a rising platform through a trap door next to my marker. I didn't know this and as I spun around I fell straight down the hole onto them. In ballet terms it was a pirouette. At that moment I didn't know what had happened to me. It was a huge shock. The ground just disappeared and I was on my back wondering what the fuck had happened. For a terrifying second I thought there had been an earthquake or bomb. I was in agony and completely confused but no one will ever know because in true fabulous style, after a few dazed seconds, I got up and carried on like falling down was all part of the fun. When you watch it back, you can see people in the audience gasping (and then laughing). It took every ounce of diva strength in me to front it out. Of course I was embarrassed, but the reason I was so embarrassed was because Arg was in the audience. And I could also see the funny side of it too.

Worse than the actual fall were the after-effects. As I stood with the winners onstage, laughing about it, I could feel a warm trickle down my leggings. I wet myself through the sheer shock of it all. I had to rush and go and do a live segment with Rita Ora and Grimmy and still perform on camera with urine in my knickers. To top it all off, when I came away from the filming bit, Arg was standing there. He looked at me full of admiration and said: 'I can't believe that happened.' I was looking at him and he was looking back at me like I was a living legend and I'm like: 'I've fancied this bloke for years and now he's seen me catapult through a stage.' We both laughed but I was still in shock. I was worried that people would be able to smell me. I had to hang around and do a bit of networking, but I got rid of Arg because I was embarrassed. I was wandering around trying to work out how to change myself when I bumped into Stormzy in the corridor and he wanted a chat. Then I got shown through to the green room (which is where the guests hang out and relax) and Dynamo walked up and collared me to do a magic card trick. All the time I'm just thinking to myself, can they see the wet patch? I looked over and James Arthur was in the corner, who I fancy like mad. It should have been one of the best days of my life but all I could think was, I need to change my knickers.

In the end I sorted myself out and left. On the way home, I needed a drink so I stopped off at one of my favourite restaurants, Sid's in Ongar, and I had a really good bottle of wine and a lobster.

It became legendary. It was my Madonna moment, like the time she fell over when one of her dancers yanked her cape. Many celebs would have been broken by such an accident but I embraced it. I've got a sense of humour. I can see how funny it was. I always look for the positives and the footage of the fall went global and made me even more of a star. My clothes choice for the day was inspired because the leggings hid the fact that I'd pissed myself. And it was worth the pain because Arg looked at me like I was a legend that day.

Wardrobe malfunction

And then of course there's 'that dress'. Every diva has a 'that dress' moment and mine happened when I was going to the ITV Summer Party. I'd ordered in something special because I wanted to stand out. Like I said before, a diva doesn't do wallflower. The room knows when a diva walks in. Part of creating that impact is having the right look.

The dress turned up, I took the cover off, had a peek and liked what I saw. It wasn't orange; it was a softer nude colour with gold chain piping around it and impressive shoulder pads. It looked classy. I hung it up and didn't think any more about it until it was time to put it on.

I'm the world's worst when it comes to time-keeping (it's a diva's prerogative to be late) so I was rushing around sorting myself out. I did my hair and make-up because once the hair and make-up is done, you stick a dress on and the rest will follow. I liked the shoulders. I felt like someone from *Dynasty*. It was a real eighties-style power dress. If you saw it on me in the cold hard light of day it actually looked amazing. The aim of the look I was going for was eighties glamour and I did my hair like one of the girls from *Charlie's Angels* (an eighties TV show with glamorous female detectives for those too young to remember) to complement the look. I was happy with the full package and left to go to the party.

When I got there, the venue was a short walk from where the guests were dropped off and there were paps hanging around. Nothing unusual in that. You go to these types of party and expect it. It's good for the profile and good for the TV company. You don't want to be the celeb who doesn't attract any photographers because that is a pretty good indication that your career is in trouble. The paps saw me and started clicking. I had a laugh with them and went on my way. But paps being paps get me every time and they managed to get the worst picture of me, taken at such an angle that it made my shoulders seem wider than they were and my head smaller than it is. There were other pictures taken at the same time, but from a slightly different angle and I look great in them. But no one wants to print those ones so the big-shoulders-small-head photos went out into the world instead and before I'd even had my first glass of bubbles they started to become a meme that went viral.

I was still in the dress while people on the other side of the world were forwarding tweets saying I look like an NFL player. At one point, my mate called and said: 'Have you seen the internet? You've gone viral.'

I laughed my head off. I thought it was hilarious. I even suggested that the NFL should give me a contract.

That day I was more embarrassed about meeting Freddie Flintoff at the party and confusing him with Peter Crouch. I bowled up to him and said: 'All right, Peter, how's Abby?' When he pointed out my mistake I wanted the ground to open up and swallow me – like it did at the Teen Awards.

The memes carried on for days and went all round the world. It was another win as far as I was concerned. The dress did what I wanted it to do. It made an impression.

The basics

I've made my mistakes so you don't have to. If I can help just one trainee diva avoid some of the things I've overcome, then it's all been worth it. The key point that every diva must remember is that you should never take yourself too seriously. You will fuck up in life, we all do, but it's how you handle those fuck-ups that makes you who you are.

Top tips:

★ Don't be afraid to fail and when you do, learn lessons for failure.

★ If you are unsure about an outfit, ask a friend's advice.

★ Dare to be different.

★ Stick by your principles, even if they make you unpopular.

★ Have a go, even if you are scared or you bruise your boobs.

★ Face adversity with a smile.

★ Look for traps, and the trap doors.

Chapter Twelve

IF I RULED THE WORLD:
THE GC MANIFESTO

I don't follow politics because it's so boring. Every politician looks the same and sounds the same and they all talk crap as far as I'm concerned. So I reckon it's time for a diva revolution and I'm going to be the one to start it. There's no reason why divas shouldn't rule the world and shake things up, because most people are bored with things the way they are. Everyone craves a bit of glamour and with divas in charge, the world would be a fabulous place.

On the following pages, I've listed the rules for the new diva dawn.

The GC for Queen

Don't get me wrong, I love the Queen. She's done wonders for this country, but bless her socks, she's really getting on now and probably fancies putting her feet up and letting someone else have a go. The choices are Prince Charles or someone completely new. Again, I've got nothing against Charles and I'm sure one day we'll meet and he'll love me. But I reckon it's time for a change in the royal boardroom. It's time for the Essex lineage to take over. Let me reign this country and it will start a new age of fabulousness. It will be the Glitter Age and the sun will always shine. I'll make sure of it because I've read up on a bit of science and apparently you can change the weather by firing tiny particles into the atmosphere. If I were queen I'd station glitter cannons all along the Essex coast to fire golden glitter into the sky to keep the rain away.

Cool Britannia

The nation needs a bit of a diva makeover and to start off with, it's time to spruce up some of our national monuments. Buckingham Palace will be first. It's an impressive building but would look even more impressive in a nice bright fuchsia colour. I'd have a go at the interior too. I've not been inside yet but I imagine it's wall-to-wall dark Farrow and Ball with heavy, dusty curtains. Some nice statement wallpaper and light sparkly voile curtains would freshen things up. The royal guards wouldn't need those huge bear-fur hats any more because they'd all have blow-dries and big hair.

The pound would get a makeover too. Obviously I'd be on the notes in a range of glamour poses and on the back we'd have a selection of divas. Marilyn would be on the £50 note and I'd probably put Mum on the fiver to keep her happy. Each note will be a different shade of pink, and some will have glitter and crystals. The pound will be so popular, everyone in other countries with boring currency will want to adopt it and collect it, so it will increase in value, making the UK economy strong and stable (honestly, I don't know why the Chancellor hasn't worked this stuff out already). The glamour will spread to everyone.

I'd do away with those stupid passport rules as well. Everyone will be able to choose their best selfie and use that on their passports instead. Shades and fascinators will be obligatory in passport photos and police mugshots. Hairy legs will be banned and possession of them will be a criminal offence. There will be an amnesty on straighteners. Anyone who owns a set will be able to hand them in without fear of ridicule or arrest and will be sent for compulsory hair re-education. Essex will become the party capital while London will remain the administrative capital. Selfridges will become the official supplier of garb to the royal household. The UK will welcome divas from all other nations with open arms but they will only get citizenship after they've taken a nationality test that will comprise solely of questions based on episodes of *TOWIE*.

National Happy Service

Positivity and bronzer will be given out on prescription on the NHS. Everyone who is feeling a bit down will be given an *Only Fools and Horses* box set. Immediate measures will be taken to spread some happiness through the nation. The first change towards this will be the title music to the news. I mean, fuck me, how depressing is it? As soon as you hear it you get a sense of dread and think the world is going to end. Newsreaders will also be forced to lighten up; most of them look like they are about to deliver some bad news about a beloved family pet. It is engineered to make people miserable. The news will be good and will be introduced with a happy little jingle. Even the bad news will be delivered with a positive pay-off: 'Good evening, everyone, today this bad thing happened in the world, but we are not going to let it get us down. Things are happening and we are going to get them sorted, but in the meantime, here are some memes of kittens.' Life can be depressing enough, especially when you are not a diva, so why make it worse by telling people stuff that will upset them?

Happy diva day

More good news, folks. I will make a new bank holiday. It will be called August. The whole of the month will be a paid holiday (funded by the rise in the value of the pink pound). The air force will use every vehicle at its disposal to organise a mass airlift to Marbella where the royal household will take up residence for the summer. While everyone is away enjoying their free holiday, I will start work on an ambitious building project and turn the whole of Hertfordshire into Gemmawood (based loosely on Dollywood, the theme park Dolly Parton built in honour of herself). The centrepiece of Gemmawood will be a huge pool with a crystal mosaic of my face in the bottom of it. There'd be a Murano glass slide going into it and chocolate fountains in place of water fountains. All the trees will be topiary of me and there will be thousands of pink flamingos everywhere. Each night Gemmawood will host a banging outdoor pool party and finish with a firework display.

Diva diplomacy

Diva Britain under The GC reign will enjoy a new era of global influence and power. Our diva diplomats and diva entrepreneurs will spread style advice and influence throughout the world which in turn will drive a global demand for British fashion and create a manufacturing boom in designer shoes and bags. Me, Mariah and Madonna will get together and form a global political alliance that will replace the UN. Donald Trump will be so grateful for the hair advice that I give him on my first official state visit to Washington that he'll make me honorary queen of Hollywood. Everyone will be happy and divas will finally rule the world.

So there it is. Come on, sisters, now you've read the guide and know the basics, it's time to rise up and throw off your chains. Replace them with some lovely Swarovski costume jewellery, maybe accessorised with a nice Pandora charm bracelet. Be divas. Start the change!

EPILOGUE

So girls, our journey together may be ending, but your journey as a diva is just beginning. And look how far you've come. When you picked up this book, I bet you were a timid little thing, pale and weak like a newborn foal. Now look at you: you're a beautiful, bronzed unicorn ready to fly across the world, spreading glitz and glamour with rainbows under your feet. I'm proud of you, babes. I hope we've shared some laughs and some secrets along the way and I hope you understand now what being a modern-day diva is all about.

The secret formula is pretty complicated but what you need to remember all the time is confidence, self-belief, courage to get what you want, bronzer, blow-dries and a sense of humour.

Stick with these to begin with and all the other stuff will start to come naturally.

It may take a bit of practice at first and you may be feeling nervous about being a diva in public for the first time. And that's OK because it can be quite nerve-wracking to begin with. Just remember to believe in yourself. You'll probably be feeling a little bit like I felt when I was first in *TOWIE*. It was all new and I was the newbie. I didn't know how it was going to work out. I got told they wanted me in the show and on my first day's filming I went to work in the BMW showroom and Kirk Norcross, whose dad Mick owns the Sugar Hut, turned up. Honestly, I was bricking it and I couldn't speak. The girl with bags of confidence was actually bottling it. It was a new experience so in the moments that followed, although I didn't understand what was happening at the time, I started to channel my inner diva. I said: 'Pull yourself together, Gem,' and I got this sudden shot of confidence.

The following day I did a scene in Faces nightclub and I was greeted by two very pretty blonde girls, Billie and Sam Faiers. I felt like the new girl at school. It was there that The GC first started to rear her beautiful head and she came out with the classic line: 'I love the geezers; it's all about being a geezer.' Once I'd clicked into diva mode I started to love it. I knew I had made the right decision. The first time I was on TV a friend, Hazel, threw a *TOWIE* party for me at hers. She put on a lovely spread. She had the carrot cake from Costco, she'd done the works. She got me pink glitter *TOWIE* balloons.

Before it came on my friend Alannah told me I needed to set up a Twitter account because people will start tweeting me. I didn't know what it was or what tweets were, but I set one up anyway. Before the show came on I had a couple of brandies to steady my nerves. When my first appearance came on everyone cheered at the TV. Twitter went mad and by the time the show ended I had about 2,000 followers.

I was too hyped to sleep that night and managed to drop off in the early hours. I woke when a friend called and told me to turn on Radio 1. I did, and Scott Mills was talking about me on his show saying I was his favourite newbie. From there everything snowballed. I had a great response as you can imagine – the house phone was going the whole of the next day, people were phoning and talking to my mum. It was a massive day in our lives. Dad took no notice, bless.

The first time I got recognised I was in a petrol station filling up my Beamer. Some bloke called over. At that point I didn't go around saying I was famous, I said I was a TV personality. But since then I've become more than famous; my life has changed in ways I couldn't have imagined. I get mobbed wherever I go. I've done loads of shows, I've flown around the world, I've met other legends, I've even been on *The Generation Game*. And there is still so much more I want to do.

I plan to carry on building my business empire until its reach is global, and I will have a chain of international boutiques and will redefine fashion for larger ladies. In the process I'll become even more of a style icon than I already am. I'll also have a range of interiors, so divas everywhere can create their own diva havens.

I'll act in Hollywood movies and I will take to the stage to fulfil my destiny as a musical leading lady, at which point hopefully The JC will finally be satisfied.

And I might settle down, have a family and get hitched – we'll have to wait and see about that one.

That's my future. What about yours? Now you've got the spirit of the diva running through your veins, there's no limit to what you can achieve. It's time for you to put this book down, give your hair a blow-dry, apply the bronzer, pick out a kick-arse outfit and a pair of killer heels and go out into the world and be fabulous. Good luck, babes, I'm with you all the way x

QUIZ

How much of a diva are you?

You are getting ready for a date and want to look amazing. How long is it acceptable to make your date wait for you?

    a) I'm never late. Punctuality is important.

    b) Thirty mins, max.

    c) For as long as it takes. I'm worth waiting for.

You are in a bar with your friends and a geezer offers to buy you a drink. Do you order:

    a) Sparkling water.

    b) Prosecco.

    c) LP Rosé all round for me and the girls. Now off you go, we're having a boogie.

A friend introduces you to her new fella at a dinner party she's hosting. Last night you saw him snogging someone in the Sugar Hut. Do you:

    a) Keep it quiet and hope he doesn't hurt her.

    b) Wait until you see her the next day and tell her.

    c) Pull her aside quietly. Explain what you saw then throw him out and comfort her for the rest of the evening.

On a work's team-building weekend you are told that as part of the course, you will be required to walk over hot coals. You have just had a pedicure. Do you:

    a) Do it then wear an unflattering pair of trainers the rest of the weekend to cover the scorch marks.

    b) Walk over them but claim for a treatment in the hotel spa afterwards on expenses.

    c) Refuse and tell the boss where to go.

Your partner has been shopping and has bought a woven tartan throw for the living-room sofa that clashes with the colour scheme. Do you:

    a) Use it anyway because it was such a sweet thought.

    b) Ask for the receipt and change it.

    c) It wouldn't ever happen. He's been well trained and knows better than to interfere with the soft furnishings.

You walk into a restaurant and the maître d' asks where you want to sit. Do you:

    a) Head to a quiet table at the back.

    b) Tell him it doesn't matter as long as the food is good.

    c) Go straight for the window seat so everyone can see you.

You win straighteners in a raffle. Do you:

    a) Take them home and sleek your hair down until it's as flat as a sheet of paper.

    b) Decline and offer them back for someone else to win.

    c) Take them home and destroy them because the world is better for having one less set of straighteners in it.

A man sends you an uninvited dick pic. Do you:

    a) Send him a pic of your vajazzle in return.

    b) Call the police and tell his wife.

    c) Get the bloke in PC World to use an animation app on it and turn it into a meme.

At work you are asked to do a presentation about the future of the business. Should you concentrate most on:

a) The projected growth within the sector.

b) Whether to invest or downsize.

c) Your outfit.

You are packing for a short two-day break and your cabin bag is almost full. What do you leave at home?

a) Bronzer.

b) Cabin baggage? I've got two cases for the hold.

c) Not my problem. My stylist packs for me so he'll sort it out. I've chartered a jet anyway, so I'll take what I want.

Scores

Mostly a

Oh dear. You really haven't been paying attention, have you? Go back to page one, start again and make notes this time.

Mostly b

You're showing promise. There is definitely diva potential there and if you keep at it, you are going to become a first-class diva graduate.

Mostly c

You go, girl! Welcome to the world of fabulousness. You get top marks. You know what you want and how to get it. You are a diva.

ACKNOWLEDGEMENTS

Thank you to Mark Thomas, my manager, and to everyone at Headline for letting me spread the diva word.

Thank you to Nick Harding for being my co-diva.

Thank you to my family and closest friends for believing in the power of the diva! Love you all.